M

I H...

Con...

Seven St...
Differences Wi...

LEE R/

New York   Chicago   San Franc
Milan   New Delhi   San Ju

Library of Congress Cataloging-in-Publication Data

Raffel, Lee.
    I hate conflict! : seven steps to resolving differences with anyone in your life / by
Lee Raffel.
        p.   cm.
    ISBN 978-0-07-148489-3 (alk. paper)
    1. Conflict management.   I. Title.

HM1126.R34   2008
303.6'9—dc22   2007030276

1 2 3 4 5 6 7 8 9 10 11 12 13 14 15 16 17 18 19 20 21   FGR/FGR   0 9 8

ISBN 978-0-07-148489-3
MHID   0-07-148489-2

McGraw-Hill books are available at special quantity discounts to use as premiums and sales promotions or for use in corporate training programs. To contact a representative, please visit the Contact Us pages at www.mhprofessional.com.

This book is printed on acid-free paper.

This book is dedicated to the memory of my beloved husband, Mark Raffel, and in memory of my dear friend Karen Bookstaff.

Contents

Acknowledgments

A book does not come together without assistance from professional and lay people alike. My heartfelt thanks goes to my agent, Denise Marcil, who has stood by me with her much-needed advise and feedback for the past twelve years. Thanks also goes to Maura Kye-Casella of Denise Marcil Agency, who was immensely helpful with the final book.

I had the pleasure of working with three highly skilled freelance editors. Elizabeth Barrett helped in the early stages of preparing my initial book proposal. Beth Lieberman expertly collaborated with me to finalize the proposal that McGraw-Hill accepted. My deepest appreciation goes to gifted Nellie Sabin, who revised the final manuscript and made it flow in a way that far surpassed my expectations.

The staff of McGraw-Hill has been incredibly supportive. I am most grateful to John Aherne, astute Senior Editor for his remarkable insights and guidance. Thanks also to Senior Project Editor, Nancy Hall who provided immense assistance. It has been a pleasure to work with these qualified professionals.

Many thanks to my resourceful assistants, Elizabeth Teeters, Joan Taylor, Adrian Hackl, Carolyn Washburne, and Lynne Barber for their efficient help. And to my daughters, Holly Bern and Laurel Bern; my husband Mark's daughters, Cherie Raffel and Dawn Raffel; and my grandson, Cale Israel, who all gave me important feedback and support. My sincere appreciation goes to my son-in-law, Shimon Israel, who provided ongoing technical support. And also thanks to Pam Bratz, Gary Schmit, and Alex Peterson who pitched in to provide expert computer and printer assistance.

Many dear friends shared their critiques and much-needed wisdom: Ellen Bank, Kay Doig, Patricia Classon, Martha Stone, Diane Forman, JoAnne Herbst, Linda Barkwill, Rose Mishlover, and Kathy Plier who helped me in so many ways. I am most grateful to my clients and friends, named and unnamed, who shared their conflict stories and enriched this book; their help warms my heart.

Endless thanks and blessings to all.

Introduction

For as long as I can remember, conflict has made me feel agitated and distressed. Ever since I was a child, I feared that my parents wouldn't love me if I upset them. I was afraid my teachers would be mean to me if I got out of line. Any kind of conflict made my body tremble and my knees turn watery and weak as if I didn't have a leg to stand on. As a lover of harmony and quiet, my heart would start racing whenever my parents fought. During my lengthy abusive first marriage, I played the role of nurturer and martyr, putting my husband and children first and myself last in the interest of keeping the peace at any price.

It took a new beginning for me to revisit old issues, gaining a more realistic perspective on what can and cannot be reasonably expected in the face of the vast dimensions and perplexities of personal and interpersonal conflict. It took my second marriage, twenty-four years with Mark, the love of my life (he died December 12, 2000), to glean new insights about conflict. Of course, Mark and I had our struggles and our disagreements because we didn't always perceive issues or approach situations the same way, but we persisted and learned how to forge a gratifying relationship. We were far from perfect, but we trusted each other. We were loving, cooperative, compassionate friends who believed in each other's worth.

The challenge of conflict touches young and old in every facet of life. The seeds for this book were firmly planted the day my client Roy suddenly shouted, "I hate conflict!" It was the force and venom in his voice that resonated with me. I thought about my childhood and how I had spent a large part of my life being terrified of conflict. I also thought of the times I had stood up for myself, stated my case, and made significant changes for myself and the world around me.

Personally, I am a peacekeeper at heart, and so was Mark. However, the more I thought about how much I have hated conflict, the more I realized that trying to avoid disagreements and confrontations simply is not a successful approach to life.

Conflict permeates every nook and cranny of our lives. We experience controversy with our loved ones, friends, relatives, and coworkers. We see conflict in movies, television, and theater. We read about conflict in books, newspapers, and magazines and on the Internet. We are beset by wars that we do or do not want. In government, industry, and politics, we see a mix of cooperation, honesty, trust, and reciprocity, as well as arrogance, corruption, greed, and retaliation. Like it or not, we are living on a sorely conflicted planet.

As a relationship expert for more than thirty-five years, I now have a clearer understanding of how, with the best of intentions, we often put our most valued relationships in jeopardy. Inadvertently, naively, blindly, we step on the toes of our loved ones and peers, and if we don't know how to handle conflict, we don't know how to rectify the damage. When we aren't prepared to address our conflicted issues, we get more heartache than we ever anticipated.

Almost all of the people I have interviewed, men and women alike, tell me they hate conflict because they are afraid to say or do anything that might harm their relationships or make a situation worse than it already is. Mismanaging conflict can spread discontent like wildfire. However, avoiding conflict altogether can cause misunderstandings to grow to immense and harmful proportions.

- "I hate conflict—someone is always getting hurt." (woman, sixty-three years old, executive assistant)
- "I don't like conflict. Who does? What should I do, just creep away?"(man, seventy-five years old, retired physician)
- "I know I shouldn't, but I sweep a lot of conflicted stuff under the rug." (woman, thirty-seven years old, homemaker)
- "Conflict sometimes makes me say things I don't want to say." (man, forty-five years old, engineer)

It isn't the conflict itself that is the issue but rather the way we perceive and manage it. The purpose of this book is to address the conflict that exists in your life and what you can do about it. If your marriage or partnership is toxic, your children are frightened, or your relationships with your parents, extended family, workplace pals, or friends have been poisoned by your ineffective efforts to handle conflict, there is hope.

I have counseled, coached, and mediated between hundreds of individuals, couples, and families, and the strategies that worked best for my clients also worked for Mark and me, so I am speaking from both personal and professional experience. We all can learned how to forge healthier relationships in all areas of life.

The central premise of this book is my belief that conflict can be a catalyst, the energy source that gives you an opportunity to deepen your relationships, to clarify your priorities, and to bring more ease and joy into your life. Despite your initial trepidation, you will discover safe and sane ways to manage your painfully conflicted relationships and learn how to become friends, not enemies.

I Hate Conflict! discusses the Mischief-Makers (for example, sarcasm and deception) that introduce stress into your relationships, as well as the inner sources of conflict that are hardwired into many of us (for example, a deep-seated fear of abandonment). The book explains my original five conflict styles, plus my all-important seven steps to managing conflict constructively and my twenty core truths to help your conversations move in an affirmative direction. The final chapters show you how to keep conflict from escalating unnecessarily, how to confront with confidence, and how to handle various types of Conflict Sabotage (for example, the silent treatment and changing the subject).

This practical book is designed to broaden your perspective of conflict. You are encouraged to look inward to better understand yourself, learn from your mistakes, and develop new ways of viewing your relationships. The unique tools and strategies in the text are designed to expand your point of view and to help you see how others influence your life. You will learn to make conflict your friend and to view with compassion the many different sides of the irritating issues that plague you. Each chapter includes case histories, sample dialogue, questions for reflection, and journal activities to ensure that you will understand new ways of viewing conflict and build them into your life successfully.

Please take note that the following addictions are beyond the scope of this book: violence, alcohol, drug abuse, eating disorders, gambling, and pornography. I have included client stories to dramatically illustrate how people have used the tools included in this book to constructively manage the conflicts that came their way. The names of my clients and most of my friends have been changed to protect their privacy.

As you go through this book, keep the following in mind:

- Everyone, including you, is imperfect and will goof up some of the time.
- Practicing the techniques in this book with a partner will invigorate and strengthen all of your relationships.
- Sharing your new insights and understandings about conflict with others will help you become better acquainted with them.

- It is more effective to focus on what works for the good of your relationships than to dwell on what is wrong.
- Using available community resources, learning from other self-help books, and attending relevant growth workshops or retreats can optimize your sense of well-being.

You now have an opportunity to redefine and reinvent yourself. In turn, you'll promote self-healing and effect changes that will help you grow closer to your loved ones. As you practice the strategies from this book, you'll have a real-life opportunity to say and do what you never dreamed you would be brave enough to say or do. Now is your time to make a significant difference in your life and close relationships.

I hope you will pace yourself as you read this book. It is not the kind of book to rush through. Take your time. Savor the experience. Take a week or two to practice one new skill or strategy at a time and see if it works for you. If a particular technique doesn't seem to be working, be patient. Let it go and try another strategy. Don't give up if things don't work out the first few times. Change is often tentative and awkward, as the results are not always predictable. If you are sincere about wanting to manage your conflicts constructively, you will profit from this book. Keep it handy as a ready reference. When you are unsure of yourself, reread certain sections that apply to your particular issues. Remember, your potential for growth and for gaining new insights, understandings, and inspiration is never-ending.

May you experience a renewal of energy from speaking up and confronting others. May you feel more secure knowing you are being your authentic self. May your continued growth offer you opportunities for lightening your load, enhancing the quality of your life, finding inner peace, and reaping much joy.

Conflict 101

Do you avoid conflict at all costs? Do you refuse to discuss problematic issues? Do you deny conflict and pretend it doesn't exist? Do you sweep it under the rug, even though you know you shouldn't? Do you try to keep the peace at all costs, only to find that it isn't possible? Are you flexible or rigid? Do you hold your ground or capitulate? Have you ever unwittingly created even more conflict than you might have initially imagined? So many questions to contemplate. No wonder conflict is so confusing!

Webster's New World College Dictionary, Fourth Edition, has a detailed, complex definition of *conflict*:[1]

1. To fight or struggle, battle, contend.
2. To be antagonistic, incompatible or contradictory, sharp disagreement, be in opposition, as of interests and ideas; clash.
3. Emotional disturbance resulting from a clash of opposing impulses or from an inability to reconcile impulses with realistic or moral considerations.
4. Synonym: any contest, quarrel, heated verbal strife or dispute, a fight or struggle for existence, either friendly or hostile, for supremacy—a contest of wits.

Emotionally, this definition of *conflict* is intimidating because you might be wondering how your moral imperative to be right and to do right is feasible when your relationships are deadlocked and you are at your wit's end. Judging from Webster's definition, you have your work cut out for you. Much depends on what you are willing to sacrifice, tolerate, condone, compromise, forfeit, negotiate, accept, reciprocate, forgive, and pardon.

What Are Your Options When There Is Disagreement?

Whenever an important issue comes up, opinions may differ, which could lead to conflict. What different courses of action are open to you? First and foremost, mind your manners, stay calm, and think clearly about the direction you want to take. Whether you hate conflict or relish it, you have the choice of taking a hopeful, optimistic path or of getting lost on a pessimistic trail. You have the following six options:

1. **Agree to agree.** You accept the solution, or in any case you let the matter be resolved by not putting any more negative energy into it. The resolution is positive for everyone. For example, two people agree on a movie they would both like to see, or one person decides and the other person doesn't care enough one way or the other to argue about it. Unfortunately, this outcome seldom works for complex issues.

2. **Compromise.** Neither side is completely satisfied, but you settle your differences in a dignified manner. Whenever there is disagreement, this option is the most equitable and paves the way for lasting cooperation going forward.

3. **Wait and see.** Waiting can be a constructive approach if you believe something may change in your conflicted situation.

4. **Agree to disagree.** This means you have a nonnegotiable issue that must be resolved, and only one person decides the outcome of the conflict.

5. **Go nowhere.** This occurs when you are polarized and you don't know how to get unstuck. The conflicted issue remains in limbo.

6. **Give up and walk away.** You decide to leave your job, move to a different state, give up a friendship, or no longer be so closely involved. This is not a resolution but a termination of the conflict. There is always the possibility you will change your mind. If you hate conflict, you may habitually go down the path of least resistance. This will keep the peace in the short term, but it sets the stage for simmering resentment and major blow-outs in the long term.

No matter how much you dislike conflict, disagreements are here to stay. You can't shut your eyes and hope conflict will disappear, because it won't. Relationships are difficult for many reasons, some of which have to do with other people's foibles, and some of which have to do with your own. Although conflict can be painful, it also can be extremely rewarding, as you'll see in the chapters ahead.

Making Conflict Your Ally

The way you approach conflict can ruin or save your relationships. The way you speak to others, what you say to them, and how you conduct yourself opens the door to sensible conversations and satisfactory solutions or to despicable, hurtful arguments that are never successfully resolved. When there is conflict but you behave in a reliable way and are responsible for your actions, your relationships thrive and grow beyond your expectations.

When two or more people interact, the potential for running headlong into conflict is very real. The challenge is to learn how to tactfully and diplomatically practice simple strategies that improve your communication and preserve your integrity. It is work, but when you resolve your differences in a dignified manner, the benefits are substantial. Although conflicts make us uncomfortable, they place us at the cutting edge of personal and interpersonal growth. When we learn to manage them in a constructive way, our rewards are positive, clear, supportive relationships.

We cannot escape conflict, because each of us is different. We don't think alike; even identical twins have separate identities. Information on coming to terms with your conflicted self, understanding how the audacious misuse of power undermines your relationships, and learning how to communicate, confront, negotiate, and achieve peace of mind is the essence of this book. Whether you hate conflict or relish it, remember that your vast experiences and differing perceptions of conflict add spice to your life.

Why We Hate Conflict

Some people actually enjoy being argumentative, but given that you picked up a book called *I Hate Conflict!* I'm assuming you are not one of them. You probably find conflict emotionally upsetting, partly because of your own angry feelings, and partly because you are hurt when other people say terrible things to you. Conflict is also frightening because it can bring permanent change. When arguments are handled poorly, relationships can be damaged or destroyed.

The problem here actually is not the fact that a conflict exists but the way we handle it. People lack the skills they need to deal with disagreements in an amicable, successful way. Day after day, as my clients share their problems and predicaments, I see evidence that people will go to great lengths to avoid conflict because they do not have the tools they need to handle difficult situations constructively.

- She said, "My dad and I have a so-so relationship. I'm intimidated by his short fuse. When he rants and raves, I ignore him until he settles down."
- He said, "I have to be supercautious about what I say to my mother because she jumps all over me if I don't agree with her."
- She said, "I don't confront my boss because I don't want to upset him—or myself."
- He said, "My sister and I have a hard time getting along, and when we fight we both get really mad. Then we don't talk for a while."
- She said, "I can't get a handle on what my mother wants from me, but I could never ask."

So often, people need to talk, but they don't know how. Instead, they tiptoe around problem issues and difficult individuals, hoping somehow a miraculous change for the good will occur all by itself. It's a happy thought, but honestly, what do you think the chances really are for something like that happening?

Walking on Eggshells

When you are afraid of his sinister look, her surly glance, his haughty know-it-all demeanor, or her chilling silence, you are walking on eggshells.

- You are frightened by your boyfriend's intimidating threats, bullying, and coercion, but you feel powerless to argue with him.
- You dread your wife's angry verbal attacks because she is so insulting and you don't want to get down on that level.

- Your body trembles when your boss is annoyed with you. His knee-jerk reactions upset you so much that you keep your distance.
- You try to be extra careful because you have a jealous girl-friend, and she'll start screaming if she gets the wrong idea.
- You can't forget your husband's aggressive assaults, which make you too upset to think clearly.
- You don't want to set off your teenage daughter again because you might not see her for days.
- You know your coworker isn't pulling her weight, but you dread the conflagration that will occur if you say anything.

When you are scared out of your wits, you don't know how to even begin fixing the problem. You feel like faulting the other person and laying the blame on him or her, but that is not a good position from which to try to make amends. You are vexed that you are being misunderstood, and it feels like nothing short of yelling will get your point across. However, you are afraid of making the other person mad and of possibly experiencing rejection or retaliation as a result. You are frustrated that you are so powerless in this situation, yet at the same time you fear letting the lid off your own rage. How did you ever let yourself get so browbeaten?

Some of my clients express their frustration in these ways:

- "I just say, 'Anything you want, dear.'"
- "I'm walking on eggshells, and the stress is exhausting."
- "I'm waiting for the other shoe to drop. No wonder I'm a nervous wreck!"
- "I'm not going to ruffle any feathers because I don't want to hurt anyone."
- "I know I should say something, but I don't want to make waves."
- "I don't want to stir up any more controversy than necessary."

Author Daniel Goleman uses the example of the wife who yells, "Goddam you! Come back here and be nice to me!"[2] This absurd contradictory statement implies, "Keep your distance, but come a little closer." Goleman calls this predicament engage-withdraw. Conflicted relationships are confusing when someone treats you with contempt one minute and with loving concern the next. This kind of inconsistency has you walking on eggshells because you never know what you are going to get next.

The Physical and Emotional Impact of Avoiding Conflict

Researcher Julianne Holt-Lunstad, an assistant professor of psychology at Brigham Young University, conducted a study in which 102 healthy men and women wore portable blood pressure monitors for three days. The results indicated that social interactions are often linked to a rise in blood pressure. Interestingly, the study found that ambivalent relationships caused a greater rise in blood pressure than outright hostile relationships. We get nervous and on edge in conflicted relationships because we aren't sure what to expect.[3]

The emotional impact of conflict is significant when you are walking on eggshells. You grow weary when your clashes stir up a worrisome storm of cumbersome emotions that are too hard to sort out. It's difficult to tell your loved ones how you feel about them when you are having trouble figuring it out yourself. You are so worn out by the physical, emotional, and spiritual impact of conflict that it takes a toll on your health and overall well-being.

Some people are ready to share their hurts and disappointments. However, people who hate conflict are generally reticent to talk about their resentments and deep-seated emotions. Deepak Chopra states, "In their innocence, children will tell you outright what they need, but once we become adults, we learn to mask our emotions."[4]

I've often worried about the folks who have hidden their emotions, because that is what I did for many long years. When your emotions are blocked, you are not in touch with your feelings, and logic alone is not the answer to resolving conflicts. When you honor your emotions, your perceptions change to a richer inner understanding of your truth—who you authentically are.

It is evident that many of us tread in the footsteps of generations of others who buried their emotions. I am reminded of Henry David Thoreau's legendary words, "Men live lives of quiet desperation." I imagine he tried to understand his own conflicted dilemmas as he walked in the woods, reflecting on his tortured life and suffering in silence because the stress was overwhelming.

Many people hate conflict because they don't like the way their body reacts to any kind of discord. It's downright scary to feel flushed with hot rage or icy cold angst, to be trembling and terrified about the dreaded outcome of your disputes. You might ask, "Why do I feel so terrible?" You worry about your heart palpitations and question, "Am I having a heart attack?" You are thinking, "What's going on that I feel so sick in my gut?" You are not thinking that literally your disagreements are difficult to stomach.

Intermittent and persistent conflict leaves you feeling apprehensive, agitated, unsettled, and exhausted. You might awaken in the morning weary, unsettled, or depressed, and this precipitates all kinds of psychosomatic ailments. It's not surprising if you lose your appetite, overeat, sleep fitfully, have frequent headaches, suffer painful backaches, or experience a host of other worrisome maladies. In the throes of conflict, you are irritable, impatient, perhaps belligerent. Of course, some people try to drown their miseries by abusing alcohol, illicit drugs, and/or prescription medications—an approach that has never worked.

It is evident that the emotional impact of conflict takes a significant toll on your physical health. Your unresolved conflicts inflame uncomfortable emotions. You feel guilty and distraught when you let others down because you see the conflict differently than they do. You are caught in a bind when you try to be your own person but don't measure up to your own expectations. You suffer with remorse, and the temptation to hide your shame is commonplace because you are too embarrassed to admit how you feel about your conflicted situation.

Can you simply ignore your conflicts? This might work for a while, but the cost to your well-being adds up over time. Can you take a detour around your conflicts? Perhaps in the short term you can dodge certain types of conflict. In the long term, however, the road to personal growth and satisfaction leads straight through your conflicts. Have no fear. You are about to learn the skills you need to deal directly with conflict, so you won't have to walk on eggshells for the rest of your life.

Introducing the Five Conflict Styles

After years of study, experience, and rumination, I have determined that there are five ways to approach conflict. Some people are very consistent and almost always use the same approach. Other people use different approaches in different settings. The five conflict styles will be discussed in detail in Chapter 4.

1. Conflict Avoiders would rather not argue with anyone about anything.
2. Conflict Fixers see conflict as an opportunity to get involved.
3. Conflict Goof-Ups never get it quite right.
4. Conflict Antagonists like to argue and win.
5. Conflict Innovators are prepared to address conflict in a responsible way.

Introducing the Seven Essential Steps to Managing Conflict Constructively

In addition, I have determined that there are seven essential steps to managing conflict. These steps do not have to be taken in a strictly sequential manner, but taken together they provide a foolproof structure for dealing with conflict. By starting with these steps, you will make it easier to process how you relate to your loved ones and peers when you disagree with them. The seven steps will be discussed in detail in Chapter 6.

Step 1: Speak politely; common courtesies count.
Step 2: Swallow your pride and admit your mistakes.
Step 3: Seek to understand; you have nothing to defend.
Step 4: Show compassion and keep the welfare of others in mind.
Step 5: Be honest and earn the trust others place in you.
Step 6: Never wave a red flag at a raging bully.
Step 7: Use encouragement and laughter to keep conflict at bay.

Introducing the Twenty Core Truths to Help Your Conversations

Finally, I have established twenty core truths that will help you view and manage your conflicts in new ways. Some of these may seem like a blinding flash of the obvious, but they are all significant truths that will have a bearing on your disagreements. The twenty core truths will be discussed in detail in Chapter 7.

1. Two people relate to each other four ways and more.
2. People assume they are right until they admit they are wrong.

3. You are the center of your world, but you are not the center of the universe.
4. Believing you are a victim makes you one.
5. You can think and feel at the same time.
6. Generally, most men like to fix mechanical things; most women want to fix relationships.
7. Communication is not the same as conversation.
8. Polarized, black-and-white thinking is a trap.
9. Written agreements are powerful.
10. Failure is a learning opportunity, not a time to give up and stop seeking a creative solution.
11. The Almighty gave us the capacity to laugh at our foibles so we would not get bored with our relationships.
12. If you want people to love you, then you be the leader and love them first.
13. People are doing the best they can at any given time, and if they knew better, they might consider doing better.
14. Regrettably, perfection is a wish, not a reality.
15. Trial and error is tantamount to fake it 'til you make it.
16. Reality is in the eye of the beholder, which makes it difficult to distinguish common sense from crazy-making.
17. No one is going to agree with you all the time, unless their brain is turned off.
18. When in doubt, don't do anything until you get more viable information.
19. Assumptions are like a sieve—they don't hold water.
20. For every action, be it verbal or nonverbal, there is a consequence.

Journaling

At the end of each chapter, I have included questions for reflection as well as journaling homework for you to do. In the next day or so, I want you to find or buy a notebook that will be your conflict journal in which you can record your thoughts, observations, insights, inspirations, and goals.

I can't speak highly enough about this simple tool. Give it a name, decorate it, or leave it plain. Be creative. Your journal gives you the opportunity to say anything you please without fear of judgment or retribution. Be sassy and nasty, and let it all hang out. Yell at your journal—who cares? Cry heaps! Let out all your pain and confusion. Complain, bitch, and moan if you wish. Laugh at yourself. Be who you are right now—the best and worst of you. And keep your journal private. Stash it away, but keep it handy enough to use daily. If writing is not your habit, two or three lines a day is sufficient. Suit yourself. This is for your personal growth. Share it with your counselor, if you are so moved.

Let's Get Started!

The chapters ahead present recent research and relevant information on relationship issues, including multiple strategies on how to conserve your energy as you face the complexities of managing your life and your significant relationships. The lessons to be learned herein are applicable to singles, couples, young adults, siblings, parents, stepparents, in-laws, grandparents, coworkers, friends, colleagues, and peers. Whether you are interested in personal growth or are struggling with severe conflict in your life, this book can vastly improve the quality of your life and interpersonal relationships.

2

You Can Run, and You Can Hide, but You Can't Escape Conflict!

Relationship conflict is a given. It is as much about circumstances as it is about people. We can't possibly agree with
everyone, all of the time, in every situation. Sometimes our disagreements are trivial and easily resolved. Sometimes they are
trivial but get blown out of proportion until the stakes are high
and feelings are seriously hurt. Sometimes conflicts threaten our
primary relationships—the ones that help define who we are and
what we are doing here.

At home we may disagree about who has what responsibilities,
how money should be handled, how children should be raised, how
in-laws and extended family members should be treated, and so
on. These are not insignificant issues. People are passionate about
their opinions, and if their beliefs and priorities are not respected,
they usually will seethe in silence. Sometimes complicating factors like domestic violence, addiction, affairs, and verbal abuse
are added to the mix. Life is perplexing at best, and irresponsible
behavior just adds another dimension to painful disagreements.

Workplace conflicts are important because we spend such a large part of our life at work, plus we bring our workplace miseries home with us. When there is a rigid hierarchy—someone tells you what to do, you tell the next person what to do, and so on—conflict is inevitable. Other kinds of disagreements always crop up at work, from legitimate issues about managing the business to approaching the coworker who doesn't actually do anything worth faulting.

Conflicted relationships on the home front do not involve the same dynamics as conflicts in the workplace because they reflect a different kind of attachment to others. We might be nervous and indecisive when we are buying a car, but it's a different kind of stress when we are having a heated argument with a loved one. When our familial ties are conflicted, it isn't the same as negotiating a lopsided real estate deal. Even employer–employee conflicts can rattle us physically and mentally, but (most of the time) we don't have to live with our employee or employer.

If you hate conflict, you probably try to ignore these controversies as much as possible. Unfortunately, this approach ultimately can only hurt you and others in the long run.

This chapter is devoted to a dozen everyday sources of conflict that add unnecessary strife to your life. Be on the lookout for these twelve sources of conflict, what I call Mischief-Makers; they are at the root of many of our clashes and are always associated with stress and conflict.

Mischief-Makers

These twelve negative types of behavior can be difficult to address because they are intricately connected like a chain-link fence. The troublemakers are blame, criticism, scorekeeping, competition, bias, deception, malicious gossip, meddling, vengefulness, amateur analysis, projection, and personalization.

Mischief Maker #1: Blame

When I think of blame, the image that comes to mind is the devil's three-pronged pitchfork. Blame directs its poison at yourself, your loved ones, and your life circumstances.

When disagreements arise, it takes two or more harshly defensive people to blame each other. When we blame, we nitpick at their flaws so we can lay claim to being right.

Blame fuels retaliation: "you blame me, so I'll blame you." Certainly our society condones blame in courts of law, government, politics, industry, families, schools, the workplace, sports, and entertainment. No wonder it appears in our close interpersonal connections. The more we are immersed in blaming others, the less we think about our own indiscretions. Blame is a big cop-out! It does not settle the score, nor does it resolve any of our conflicted concerns. Blame is just a way of shifting responsibility onto someone else.

The book *Difficult Conversations: How to Discuss What Matters Most* notes:

> Focusing on blame is a bad idea because it inhibits our ability to learn what's really causing the problem and to do anything meaningful to correct it. . . . Too often, blaming also serves as a bad proxy for talking directly about hurt feelings. . . . When blame is in play, you can expect defensiveness, strong emotion, interruption, and arguments about what "good assistants," "loving spouses," or "any reasonable person" should or shouldn't do. When we blame someone, we are offering them the role of "the accused," so they do what

accused people do: they defend themselves any way they can. Given what's at stake, it easy to see why the dance of mutual finger-pointing often turns nasty.[1]

Blame is an ingrained habit that has negative repercussions. Habitual blame is disastrous because it destroys any hope of reconciling and making amends. In his book *Healing the Heart of Conflict*, Rabbi Marc Gopin addresses the complexity of blame, saying:

> When we fight we tend to simplify what is going on. We resist getting too wrapped up in assigning blame fairly; it is easier to consider something all one person's or group's fault. . . . Conflict is confusing precisely because in most situations there is *not* a perfectly clear way to assign blame. It is extremely difficult for the most seasoned and moral judges to figure out who is more right in most situations—it depends on your point of view. . . . We are too busy defending ourselves or preparing our own attack.[2]

Kerry Patterson's book *Crucial Conversations: Tools for Talking When Stakes Are High* makes the important point that blaming is largely a waste of time anyway, because the only person we have any control over is ourselves.

> Most of us are quick to blame others. If others would only change, then we'd all live happily ever after. If others weren't so screwed up, we wouldn't have to resort to silly games in the first place. They started it. It's their fault, not ours. And so on.
>   Although it's true that there are times when we are merely bystanders in life's never-ending stream of head-on collisions, rarely are we completely innocent. More often than not, we do something to contribute to the problems we're experiencing.

. . . As much as others may need to change, or we may *want* them to change, the only person we can continually inspire, prod, and shape—with any degree of success—is the person in the mirror.[3]

To illustrate the consequences of blaming, I often tell my clients a fictional story.

Amy puts a glass of milk on the table, and Kent walks by and knocks the glass of milk onto the kitchen floor. Amy is furious and shouts, "What's the matter with you? Didn't you see the milk on the table?"

Kent says angrily, "Yeah, so why did you put the glass on the edge of the table?"

Amy replies snidely, "Why are you always so clumsy?"

Kent ups the ante and yells, "It was an accident, and it's all your fault for putting the glass of milk on the edge of the table!"

Amy gets on her high horse and retorts, "If you were looking where you were going, this never would have happened."

As they get louder and meaner, Kent says, "Knock it off! All you ever do is criticize!"

Amy retorts, "That's because you're an idiot!"

Meanwhile, the cat is busy lapping up the spilt milk, and to make matters worse, the dog steps in the milk and tracks it onto the brand-new living room carpet. Now no one is cleaning up the mess because the partners are too busy arguing about who is to blame.

In truth, there is a real-life postscript to this story. One day Mark put a glass of orange juice on the kitchen table. I walked by and accidentally brushed the glass, which then fell, sending juice all over the floor. I let out a shriek and was ready to pounce on Mark for putting the glass so close to the edge of the table. And then I abruptly stopped myself and started to laugh. This was a genuine déjà vu experience, because I was actually living my invented tale. I really was ready to blame Mark, and I could see us going back and forth, finding fault and hurting each other. I thought, "For what?"

Do everything in your power to banish blame. I suggest that you recall my fictional/real-life story anytime you are tempted to play "gotcha."

Mischief Maker #2: Criticism

Criticism is a first cousin to blame, as they work hand in glove together. When we blame, we are fixated on accusing others for their flaws.

Once again I turn to the dictionary, which says that criticism "implies an attempt at objective judging, so as to determine both merits and faults, but it often connotes emphasis on faults and shortcomings."[4]

Criticism begins in early childhood, when we are in dire need of discipline. Often we were scolded in a harsh manner for our naughty behavior. By the time we become adults, we have had our fill of reprimands, sarcasm, and disapproval. It's a fact of life: grown-ups don't want to be the recipient of any more faultfinding!

Often we don't take into account how hurtful our snide remarks really are. An offhand remark like "How can you be so stupid?" provokes aggravation in return. Remember that spiteful conversations belittle the other person, who then resents you. I suggest to my clients that they deliberately speak in a warm, friendly voice in order to ease the strain of a conflicted relationship.

Some people can't seem to resist the impulse to judge others in a negative manner. What apparently eludes them is that unwanted criticism is one of the fastest ways to create more conflict. Unquestionably, unwanted criticism is bad news for the health of your close relationships. *Remember, criticism is off-limits except when a critique is requested.*

My client Joy once said to me during a session, "Ever since I was a child, my mother has had a cynical attitude. I try to love her, but she's so pushy, always telling me I should date these boys that aren't my type. My mother doesn't realize how negative she can be. She's just looking at what I do wrong, and that hurts. I don't want to be depressed, so I thought it would be good if I lost a few pounds and got in shape. I joined a health club, and now I'm working out three times a week. I think the exercise is perking me up, because I feel good about doing something positive for myself. I know I can't change my mother, so I listen to her with half an ear and keep my exposure to her at a minimum."

Mischief Maker #3: Scorekeeping

Scorekeeping refers to our internal ledger whereby we secretly keep an account of all the times we were maligned and vilified and all the times we were praised and appreciated. We do this scorekeeping in the left hemisphere of the brain by adding and subtracting our traumatic events and joyous experiences.

What's wrong with keeping track? At times we forget to take into account all the good things that come our way. Furthermore, some of us are in such close touch with our internal ledger that we become injustice collectors. Instead of releasing the negative energy associated with slights and insults, we relive them every day, shining our grudges like trophies.

Theoretically, scorekeeping should provide a logical way of evaluating the state of our relationships, but there is no sensible way to keep a ledger of this type. Does one insult equal one kind gesture? Does one fabulous present make up for twenty cutting remarks? Can you balance the books at all when there has been a serious transgression?

If you must keep score, I recommend monitoring your own behavior. How often are you kind, and how often are you thoughtless? Beware: we tend to be sloppy about tallying our own blunders, unless we are obsessing about how appalling they are.

Mischief Maker #4: Competition

Competition is an extreme version of scorekeeping, as with competition, *both* adversaries keep track of who is the smartest, who is the rudest, who makes the most money, who does the least housework, who is the biggest goody-goody, who works the longest hours, who has the best garden, the fastest car, the most expensive home, or the most unruly kids at school, and so on. We live in a competitive world where there are huge disparities between the haves and the have-nots. Conflicts abound when we are envious of what others have. Be it on the home front, at the workplace, around the neighborhood, or anywhere else, competitors are rivals—they are not cooperative team players.

A friend of mine once told me a sad family story about her aunt. Ruth adored her only child, Scott. Her husband had died two years earlier, and she leaned on her son for help. When Scott married Sandra, it wasn't long before Ruth clashed with her son's new wife. Sandra disapproved of Ruth's dependence on Scott and called her a controlling busybody. Ruth complained to Scott, "Sandra's got a big sassy mouth." Sandra had a fit when Scott bought groceries for his mother. Sandra objected when Scott took his mother to the doctor and when he took her to a special concert. Sandra thought all these favors were a dreadful imposition on her, and she took her fury out on Ruth. The two women barely spoke to each other, and when they did, the sparks flew. Scott was so uncomfortable in the middle that he didn't dare confront either his wife or his mother.

Scott and Sandra had heated arguments about Ruth. One evening, with no warning, Sandra stormed into their bedroom and shrieked, "Scott, I hate Ruth! So it's your choice whether you want to be married to me or married to your mother. You better know up front that if you pick your mother, I'm leaving you!" Scott chose to be with his wife and had to really distance himself from his mother. Tragically, Ruth grieved the loss of her estranged son the rest of her life.

If only Scott had been able to deal with the conflict between these two women, they might have been able to negotiate a compromise. Unfortunately, Scott continued to avoid the problem until time fixed it for him.

Mischief Maker #5: Bias

In his book *The 7 Habits of Highly Effective People,* Stephen R. Covey explains his thoughts on *fairness:* "I am referring . . . to the principle of *fairness,* out of which our whole concept of equity and justice is developed. Little children seem to have an innate sense of the idea of fairness. . . . There are vast differences in how fairness is defined and achieved, but there is almost universal awareness of the idea."[5]

Covey is absolutely right about children's acutely developed sense of fairness. I'm sure you can remember incidents of absolutely outrageous unfairness from your childhood, such as your sister taking an extra cookie and getting away with it or your brother leaving the bicycle outside in the rain all night and your getting blamed for it. The stakes are a lot higher for adults, and inequities—including unfairness, injustice, bias, partiality, prejudice, and favoritism—can have very serious consequences. When others are not fair to us, our disputes can go clear up to the Supreme Court for resolution.

When we behave unfairly toward others, the inequity instigates more strife than we know how to handle. When we insist on having the upper hand, there is an adverse imbalance of power. One person domineers and torments, while the other meekly slinks into the shadows. When we take sides, we risk escalating a war. When we favor one child over another, we cause lifelong competition.

As a rule, we anticipate that our loved ones will treat us fairly, but do we treat them impartially? When parents, grandparents, and employers play favorites, one person is lauded and praised while others receive less or no recognition for the merits they deserve. No wonder favoritism diminishes our self-esteem.

We are often biased, whether we admit it or not. It is easy to presume that we are neutral, but usually this is a fallacy. It is difficult to be impartial when we don't understand ourselves, and we can't recognize the biases others see in us. Being subjective is one of many reasons why conflict is so complex.

We often handle conflict unfairly. In the midst of a heated verbal exchange, we may overreact and say whatever it takes to win the argument, even if it means losing the war. Tactics such as faulting others and fighting to get our own way are bound to backfire. The goal is an equitable resolution of conflict. When we are impartial and refuse to take sides, we can readily resolve our disputes. As we think about inequality, let's not forget that we are each one of a kind—and that means we must be humble and treat others in the fairest way possible.

It is interesting to note that inequity is a moving target. What we might think is unfair today can shift overnight and be gratifying tomorrow. For instance, you might win an award you didn't think you deserved or get a job that could've gone to another equally qualified candidate. In these cases, fairness takes on a different complexion because we are the ones who benefit.

Mischief Maker #6: Deception

Honesty is absolutely the most important thing in relationships. Lies and secrets destroy trust, and sins of omission (neglecting to share important information, such as that you loaned $5,000 to a friend) are as dangerous as sins of commission (telling an outright lie, such as that you spent the night at a friend's house when in fact you didn't).

Most people lie now and then, but deception is the ultimate betrayal that poisons relationships. When people lie, they take a calculated risk. Usually, they are hoping they don't get caught, although occasionally people secretly realize they need to get caught in order to bring serious issues into the open. This explains the teenager who accidentally-on-purpose leaves her journal open on her bed or the husband who says he is working late but comes home with lipstick on his collar.

My clients Janice and Ralph had a steadfast marriage for seven years. When I met with Janice, she said, "Something fishy is going on with Ralph. He seems preoccupied. He's not himself. I can't put a finger on what's the matter. When I asked him to help me reconcile our bank statements, he put me off with lame excuses. That's when I got suspicious."

I asked Janice if she had confronted Ralph with her fears, and she said, "No, not really. I asked him if he was all right, and he said, 'I'm tired. You know I've been traveling and working long hours. Don't worry, I'm OK.' I've always trusted Ralph, but my gut feeling is that something is wrong somewhere."

A week later I met with the couple. Janice had asked Ralph to come to my office with her, and he did not know how to refuse without looking suspicious. After I asked him a few questions, Ralph admitted that he had manipulated a substantial sum of money without telling Janice that he did it. Janice looked aghast.

Janice said, "Ralph, I don't understand why you deceived me! I always trusted you. Why didn't you tell me?"

At first, Ralph didn't answer. Reluctantly, he said, "I didn't want to see that mean look on your face."

I intervened by asking, "Ralph, what do you mean by 'that mean look'?"

Ralph said, "When Janice and I aren't getting along, she glowers at me and I get scared."

I wanted to know more. "Ralph, why are you so scared of Janice?"

With no hesitation, Ralph said, "I was afraid that Janice would be mad at me if she found out that I deceived her. And I didn't want to start an argument, because when we argue, it gets nasty."

Clearly, Ralph's lies and Janice's mistrust were at the heart of the conflict. The couple worked diligently by exploring the damage of suspicion and deception. Ultimately, the couple learned that to have a stable relationship, each person must be responsible for his or her own conduct. They must consistently be honest with their partner, and then gradually, they can safely trust one another again.

Mischief Maker #7: Malicious Gossip

There is a vast disparity between friendly gossip and malicious gossip. Friendly gossip is fun. This kind of casual conversation is how we keep up with news about what's going on. No one gets hurt, because everyone's in a good mood and they want to stay that way. Malicious gossip, however, is a wicked sport. What starts out as innocent chatter within the confines of a small group leads to twisted stories, half-truths, and outright lies passed among many others. Imprudent gossip is a treacherous undertaking, one that is thoughtless, hurtful, and unwarranted.

Malicious gossipers are on the outside looking in; their intention is to purposely wound you. Having friends with such a mean streak does not bode well for you, because they have betrayed you. They are extremely insensitive, spiteful, and hateful. Inasmuch as malicious gossipers are boorish, ill mannered, and inappropriate, they make utter fools of themselves in social situations. If truth is on your side, you do not need to get down to their level and defend yourself. Your reputation will speak for you, as theirs will speak for them.

Malicious gossipers tend to exaggerate and spread private information or misinformation that they haven't bothered to check out. Be cautious about taking your remarks one step too far and carelessly falling into a gossip fest, for doing so will instigate deplorable conflict. Is your comment important, or is it mere trivia that diverts the conversation and puts the focus on you? Before you engage in humiliating gossip that you will later regret, keep in mind the following guidelines:

- If your comment is cordial, then you have the green light to share it.
- If your comment is repugnant, then what benefit is there in sharing it?
- If your comment is not true, then do not say it.
- If you are embellishing, exaggerating, or conveying information that you haven't checked out, then your silence is golden.

Ideally, it's best to treasure your loyal and true friendships and purposefully ignore malicious gossipers, even when this is difficult to do. In other words, when in doubt, keep your mouth shut, and you'll maintain your dignity and self-worth.

Mischief Maker #8: Meddling

When you ask others to speak on your behalf, you are buying a bushel full of unnecessary conflict because triads are trouble. Many make the mistake of asking a third party to rescue them, not realizing they are making matters worse. Often people will send someone to sound out a situation on their behalf. ("Does he like me?" "Will she talk to me?" "Is he still mad at me?" "Has she changed her mind?") Sometimes entire families or groups of friends are intrusive and get in the middle of what should be a relatively simple, direct conversation.

When menacing meddlers get involved, be cautious about becoming entrapped in the middle of unrelenting discord. There

are safer ways to resolve your impasse than to involve nosy, intrusive folks who don't have your best interests in mind.

Troy said, "My sister is a pest! I asked my older brother to confront her because I was too uncomfortable to do it myself. It turned
out to be an awful fiasco, because my brother got the information
all mixed up and now the whole family is mad at me."

Triangulation. Sometimes third parties get drawn into your
conflicts or insert themselves in your conflicts because they enjoy
the drama. Meddlers can do nothing—I repeat, nothing—to help
you "fix" your conflicts.

Sometimes people get involved in disputes that are not their
own because they are eager to help. Inevitably, the rescuer is
someone who wants to help and who is happy to speak on behalf
of someone who is afraid of conflict. Regrettably, when a third
person intrudes and creates a triad, everyone loses.

My mother was a victim of triangulation when she fancied that
she could save her best friend's highly conflicted marriage. She
spent considerable time with the couple as their quasi-therapist,
and one evening she came home totally demoralized as the couple
found her intrusive ways unwelcome. My mother was banished
from ever seeing her dearest friend again. I was about fourteen
at the time, and that's when my "don't-get-too-close" wall went
sky-high.

Mischief Maker #9: Vengefulness

When someone hurts you and you want to hurt him or her back,
revenge is at the root of your aggressive arguments. You have a
malicious intent to retaliate and punish the other person, giving
an eye for an eye. It's just plain human nature to subconsciously
want to settle the score. However, revenge has no place in mature,
respectful relationships, particularly with loved ones. A vengeful

stance reveals a lack of caring concern. When you seek to do harm, your close relationships sink fast because no lifeguard is on duty.

Resist the temptation to strike back, because the outcome does irreparable harm to your relationships, hurting you as much as the other person. Wisdom suggests you shift your mind-set from malice to kindness and consciously decide not to undermine any of your close relationships. Revenge is said to be sweet, but seeking revenge is bitter when you are consumed with a ruthless, cynical attitude. If you hope to rise beyond revenge, you must understand that vengeance is the worst way to settle the score because you are avoiding getting to the root of your conflicted issues.

Mischief Maker #10: Amateur Analysis

Amateur analysis is another popular ploy that poisons our relationships. Conflicted conversations become contaminated when we attempt to analyze others because we are dissecting their weaknesses and faults. When we are trying to analyze our loved ones, friends, or coworkers, their smallest errors loom larger than life. Inevitably, our analysis focuses on our disapproval. We forget the wisdom of encouraging and praising others, which is sorely needed in conflicted situations. When we analyze other people's blunders, we lose sight of showing our abiding love and caring concern. This is how conflicted conversations turn toxic, and we can expect that ensuing arguments will get out of hand.

- She said, "You know what's wrong with you? Your brother always got all the attention, so now you always have to make a scene."
- He said, "Why do you have to flirt like that? I think you honestly believe losing weight made you Helen of Troy."
- She said, "The babysitter thinks you came onto her. Does this have something to do with your Napoleonic complex?"

When I began my graduate studies at the University of Wisconsin–Madison in 1971, esteemed Rabbi Manferd Swarsensky gave me a fresh perspective on the hazards of analysis when he said, "Too much analysis leads to paralysis." I've never forgotten this wisdom because it has proved to be true.

At first I was puzzled by the rabbi's words, because I had the impression that analyzing conflicted relationships was what counselors were supposed to do. As a student of psychology, I didn't understand that it is foolhardy to waste our time and energy analyzing our loved ones, our friends, or anyone else in our life because all we do is find fault with the other people, and that is the quickest way to alienate them.

I often tell my clients that none of us can see the back of our head without a mirror. It is our inability to notice what others see in us that makes it so difficult to be detached and neutral. This explains why analysis does so much harm to our closest relationships and why it doesn't make sense to waste time analyzing others. Nothing is ever resolved by analyzing because we make seven incorrect assumptions:

1. We assume we are expert enough to explore the depths of another person's behavior.
2. We believe we are objective enough to comprehend the other person's complex experiences.
3. We are sure that we are entitled to analyze another individual's foibles.
4. We suppose that our perceptions are right and the other person's observations are wrong.
5. By analyzing others, we see no need to look inward and explore our own effect on the conflict.
6. Instead of defining our own responsibility in the conflict, we assume that blame belongs with the other person.
7. We believe there will be no ramifications.

Amateur analysis, like a roaring wildfire, quickly gets out of control, because analyzing is a ploy that upsets others and shatters your potentially stable relationships. Obviously the other person is going to get defensive, so you are acting naive if you don't anticipate that he or she will twist your words around and blame you for your inexcusable behavior. Analysis is a futile undertaking, and the only place for it is in a shrink's office.

Mischief Maker #11: Projection

Projection is another futile undertaking. Projection is the process of taking your own issues and reading them into other people's behavior. The dictionary defines this kind of projection as "the unconscious act or process of ascribing to others one's own ideas, impulses, or emotions, especially when they are considered undesirable or cause anxiety."[6]

Usually, we are oblivious to the harm that projection does to our relationships. We aren't even aware we are doing it. Projections are like mistaken mind reading as we assume we know what others are thinking, when in fact our insights reflect what *we* are thinking, not what *they* are thinking. It makes no sense to imagine that you can get into another person's head.

The following are typical skewed remarks that reflect projection:

- "I know you think I don't know what you're talking about."
- "You've got it wrong, because I'm convinced you aren't hearing me."
- "I know you twist things around to suit your own convenience."
- "You're so sure that you are right, and you make me the bad guy."
- "I figure your mind is made up, so there's no talking to you."
- "You treat me like I'm stupid, I know you do."

In his book *Blink*, author Malcolm Gladwell notes, "Mind-reading failures happen to all of us. They lie at the root of countless arguments, disagreements, misunderstandings, and hurt feelings. And yet, because these failures are so instantaneous and so mysterious, we don't really know how to understand them."[7]

It is human nature to use projection because it occurs instantaneously. Like most defensive behaviors, projection happens outside our conscious awareness. Like a snap judgment, it occurs without benefit of rational thought, critical sensitivity, or discernment. We treat our ideas as if they were sacred truths carved in stone, even though we have no concrete evidence that there is any truth in what we are presupposing. Unfortunately, these assessments and conclusions substantially injure our relationships.

When two people use projection, their conversation is distorted and mixed with excuses and explanations because each person has a different agenda in mind. Each is listening not to what the other is saying but instead to what is in his or her own head. They talk *at* each other, not *with* each other. They make assumptions about each other's thoughts, motives, and likely responses. Conversations are tangential, darting from one topic to another because neither person is being forthright and honest. Neither person has thoughts of responding in a straightforward manner. If you look beneath the surface, it's apparent that each speaker has his or her version of what the other person supposedly is thinking. Neither is consciously aware of using projection. Conflicts proliferate when two or more frustrated people are scratching their heads trying to make sense of garbled conversations loaded with projections.

Projection is an easy trap to fall into, and it is harmful because we use it as an unconscious ploy to avoid looking inward and exploring our own thoughts and emotions. When we project our issues onto other people, we cannot be absolutely sure what they are thinking. Sometimes our projections are outright wacky because they are subliminal. Inadvertently, we allow our projections to mislead us down dubious paths whereby our intent to resolve our differences is deflated as soon as we open our mouth.

Mischief Maker #12: Personalization

When you personalize, you take a matter that does not necessarily have anything to do with you and make it all about you. More often than not, this causes you needless pain. If a sales clerk is rude, you may personalize the situation by taking his or her offensive words or actions to heart. This will make you respond defensively, and a conflict is born. Maybe your feelings are hurt, and the incident ruins your day. Maybe you get angry, because you feel you deserve better treatment. It's possible the sales clerk isn't feeling well and wasn't thinking about you at all.

You heap suffering on yourself when you personalize because you are borrowing another person's pain. Practically speaking, that other person's hurt and pain do *not* belong to you. We are obliged to deal responsibly with our own foibles, but when we personalize, we become burdened down with guilt and remorse because someone hurt our feelings. We personalize that this upheaval is all about us and not about them. We are angry with those who have offended us, and we are disturbed because we don't know how to right the wrongs that we assume are our problem.

When you refuse to personalize his mood or her distress, you experience a sense of freedom you never thought possible. You are at liberty to address your differences in a wiser manner. Remember, it is the other person's problem, *not* your problem. You must define your boundaries, and then you will no longer feel so wretched because of someone's supposed cruelty to you.

If you are at risk of personalizing another's behavior, here are some helpful reminders:

- Don't take another person's nasty remark as a personal affront.
- Don't allow yourself to be contaminated by another person's venom.
- You can't fix another person's pain. Your task instead is to heal your own wounds.

In his bestselling book *The Four Agreements*, Don Miguel Ruiz offers this description of the benefits of not taking things personally:

> When we really see other people as they are without taking it personally, we can never be hurt by what they say or do. Even if others lie to you . . . they are lying to you because they are afraid you will discover they are not perfect. It is painful to take that social mask off. . . . The whole world can gossip about you, and if you don't take it personally you are immune.[8]

Empathy is a completely different matter. We must be empathetic with others, acknowledging their distress. And when we recognize their pain without personalizing it, we make a significant mental adjustment. We might be sorry for others, but their wounds are not ours. We can let them know that we are there to help them when they need us, but we cannot rectify their suffering. Our obligation is to recognize our own foibles and to address them responsibly.

Questions for Reflection

Take a few minutes to reflect on the following questions:

- How do feel when another has blamed you?
- Is this person specific, or is he or she implying that you have done something wrong?
- Are you competitive with those who are close to you?
- What is usually the outcome when you blame your partner, a friend, or a coworker?
- Do you secretly keep an account of all your ups and downs?
- Do you keep better track of your miserable times than of your happy times?
- Do you personalize the ways others have hurt you?
- Do you keep track of your uplifting experiences?
- Do you feel guilty for the way you have wounded others?

Journaling

By taking time to reflect on the preceding nine questions, you began to get a handle on how you do or don't take responsibility for your own behavior. Begin writing your answers in your journal. As you write, you are apt to feel emotional and deeply hurt from your point of view. If you are prone to blaming others, write about how this affects your close relationships. If you are competitive, consider whether this makes you feel superior or inferior toward others.

Now imagine that you are the other person, and write about what he or she might be experiencing when projecting his or her thoughts on you. Note that as you explore your inner self, you expand your perceptions. The more you write about your scenarios, the more you increase your capacity for empathy, and the more you grow. This is indeed a worthwhile endeavor.

3

Hardwired Sources of Conflict

My daddy never learned how to comfortably address any kind of controversy, so he would pout. That's when he showed his daunting control-freak demeanor. Many times, living in our home was scary because he would be sulking, and my mother, brother, and I would be cringing, afraid to say anything to him because no one in our family had the language to talk about our feelings. To make matters worse, my daddy was sneaky enough to figure out how he could hold my mother, brother, and me hostage, as quite literally he controlled the uncomfortable atmosphere in our tiny apartment. This is how he did it.

In the evening, when my daddy was upset for any reason at all, he would sit on the couch and open his newspaper wide enough to cover his head and face, so all we could see was the rest of his torso. He never spoke a word. The pall was as thick as a dark cloud while we waited for him to say something, but all we ever got was dead silence. We tried to ignore him as we walked around our tiny apartment hanging our heads, but we were too intimidated to poke him or do anything to get his attention.

My father's pout was enough to tell me he was angry, but as a child I never knew exactly why. I just knew he was miserable and that made us unhappy. Even as a nine- or ten-year-old child, I thought to myself, "What a waste!" Pathetically, we were all so alone that we never comforted one another. All the while, my daddy was mute, and we were silent sufferers.

The icy silence in our home made my skin crawl. For certain, I felt rejected, waiting for my daddy's dark cloud to go away. Time dragged, though it probably was less than an hour before this unpleasant ordeal would be over. As none of us spoke a word, the atmosphere felt as if it were poisoned. I can only guess he was sending us the silent message "I feel horrible, so don't bother me. Just go away and leave me alone!" Because conversation was cut off, I was obsessed with waiting on pins and needles until he finally folded his newspaper, stood up, showed his gloomy face, and went to bed.

Memories like these are not forgotten. Like poison ivy, they grow tendrils through our psyche, and occasionally a sharp, shiny leaf will appear to remind us that our earliest experiences are always in the back of our mind. We all have inner conflicts due to past hurts. I call these hardwired sources of conflict.

The Primary Emotions: Fear and Anger

In the normal course of events, no one escapes feelings of fear and anger; these are primary emotions. Fear is the first emotion the newborn experiences. If the infant has to wait too long to be fed, then anger follows on the heels of fear. As a child, you experienced fear when you woke up in a dark room by yourself or when you encountered a threatening dog. You experienced anger when you did not get your way or when your parents were not able to immediately help you in the way you wanted.

Ideally, a warm, predictable, and consistent attachment between infant and parent or caregiver allows the baby to develop a sense of security and trust. If a parent is harsh or cruel, the infant grows up feeling insecure and mistrustful. When it comes to having difficult conversations, a fearful adult is at a disadvantage. Communication breaks down when people feel intimidated, pressured, bullied, or coerced.

Fear and anger are puzzling because rarely do we consider how these core emotions affect our well-being. Author Daniel Goleman notes that fear and anger are grounded in our ancient past:

> Our emotional legacy of evolution is the fear that mobilizes us to protect our family from danger . . . automatic reactions of this sort have become etched in our nervous system, evolutionary biologists presume, because for a long and crucial period in human prehistory they made the difference between survival and death.[1]

Just as the feelings of fear and anger are an ancient emotional legacy, so are our experiences of fear and anger from childhood a psychic legacy. It is interesting to notice that fear and anger are two sides of the same coin. Fear and anger can be linked in many ways, such as the following:

- You *fear* inciting another person's wrath, and you are *angry* because you know that person will lash back at you if you say anything.
- You *fear* being hurt, and you are *angry* because you do not want to fight back.
- You *fear* being manipulated, and you are *angry* because you detest being rebuffed and misunderstood.
- You *fear* being overpowered, yet feeling vulnerable and helpless makes you *angry*.
- You *fear* your own *anger*, and that usually stops you in your tracks.
- You *fear* retaliation, and you are *angry* at yourself for being an ineffective communicator.

When you are scared, anger lurks close behind. Fear warns you of real or potential danger, while anger prepares you to lash out and fight for your life. High stress triggers the reptilian brain—your early survival brain—in three different ways:

1. Fight. You might stand and defend yourself.
2. Flight. You might withdraw and get the hell out.
3. Freeze. You might go numb, and your brain might shut down.

The Physical Impact of Fear and Anger

Unbridled fear and anger do untold damage to body, psyche, and soul, especially when we don't let go of our hostile feelings. In the old days, stress may have involved falling into a tar pit or being threatened by a saber-toothed tiger—situations that called for immediate physical action, which was conveniently fueled by the body's stress hormones. Today stress can be an overwhelming emotional issue that has no corresponding appropriate physical response. We still have the fear and anger, and the stress hormones are ready to help us fight or flee, but no physical response is required. It's like the fire engine is ready, with the engine roaring and the siren screaming, but there's nowhere to go.

Child psychologist Barbara Kuczen points out, "Anger—or the fight response—is handled in one of two ways, either we 'pop our cork' or silently seethe." Kuczen indicates that "there is inherent danger in both of these reactions."[2]

I have experienced both forms of anger, but it took many years. When my brother, Freddie, was four years old and I was six years old, our mother would often warn us, "Now children, don't be angry!" I thought it strange that my mother and father were often angry, but for some unknown reason, we children were not allowed to show any anger. So we became expert at stuffing our bad feelings, and of course, nobody talked about that.

The Fear Continuum

The faces of fear move on a continuum from relatively benign to paralyzing. Fear can make us feel uncomfortable, worried, unsettled, intimidated, threatened, distressed, overwhelmed, panicky, and even numb.

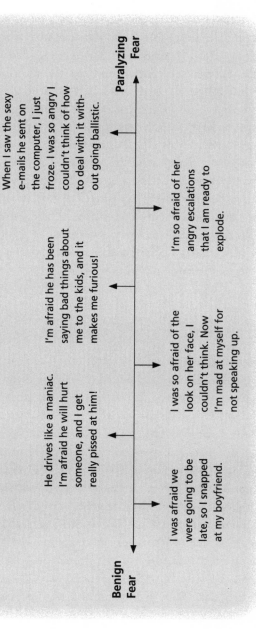

Benign Fear

I was afraid we were going to be late, so I snapped at my boyfriend.

He drives like a maniac. I'm afraid he will hurt someone, and I get really pissed at him!

I was so afraid of the look on her face, I couldn't think. Now I'm mad at myself for not speaking up.

I'm afraid he has been saying bad things about me to the kids, and it makes me furious!

I'm so afraid of her angry escalations that I am ready to explode.

When I saw the sexy e-mails he sent on the computer, I just froze. I was so angry I couldn't think of how to deal with it without going ballistic.

Paralyzing Fear

When I was ten years old, I promised myself that I wouldn't be a complainer because I was weary of my parents' daily complaints. I must admit that my thoughts were loaded with complaints, but that was my secret. Fortunately, the tedious emotional climate in our home was relieved when Freddie played the clown while Daddy was at work; our laughter helped lighten our dreary load.

As a child I wasn't aware that I showed my displeasure by pouting. Now I know that I copied this trait from my daddy. But my mother put a stop to all this when she insisted that I never leave the house without putting a broad smile on my face. My smile was so engrained that it was automatic. I smiled to everyone no matter the situation, appropriate or not. In fact, I did not experience redhot rage until I was forty-six years old—and that excruciatingly painful experience opened the door to many priceless insights that I had never known before.

Traumatic Early Experiences

Many people idealize childhood. We think of healthy, laughing, adorable, pink-cheeked children riding on carousels, picking apples, or hugging teddy bears, being doted on by their parents and siblings. We recall charming childhood games and amusements, outdoor romps and swimming expeditions, cute puppies and birthday cakes, whiskers on kittens, and all the rest.

There is also an inescapable dark side of childhood. Young children develop a fear of strangers at about the age of six months. Preschool-age children fear being separated from their parents. When parents don't get along, children are fearful and have antennae that keep them apprised of the chaotic state of their parents' conflicted relationship. Children pull the blankets over their heads because they don't want to listen to their parents' belligerent battles. They have nightmares and cry themselves to sleep, fearing they will be forced to choose between parents in the event of a divorce. Sometimes kids plot and plan how to fix conflicts with siblings or Mom and Dad. When family members do not get along, some children blame themselves for the sorry state of their family interactions. Fear of a potential family breakup often threatens the physical and emotional health of youngsters, who fear abandonment and refuse to go to school. And some kids resort to denial to insulate themselves from the pain of living in a highly conflicted family.

As children get older, they have more to fear. Some worry about a family member's dying. School-age children fear failure. Teens are prone to social fears about not being popular enough. They have sexual fears because they have the wrong information or not enough information. In general, children—and adults—have worrisome fears about their future.

There are times when your conflicted relationships are so perplexing you might be discouraged about your chances of successfully resolving them. If you can't understand why your relationships are so difficult, consider your past and present fears, such as those of rejection, abandonment, betrayal, or neglect. These fears, based on your earliest life experiences, are the root source of many conflicts. Understanding them can shed some light on your current interactions. At the same time, it is important not to let past hurts unfairly influence present relationships.

Fear of Rejection

Fear of rejection is one of the most pervasive fears, but it really is fear of the pain of rejection. Imagine when you were a child that someone thoughtlessly said to you, "Oh, no, not *you* again!" You were cut to the quick, but no doubt you pretended not to care. Later, when a clique or a club or a team didn't want you as a member, you vowed that it made no difference to you—but deep down the rejection hurt badly. It felt like a reflection of your worth. Your parents may have told you that there are a million different clubs and teams to join, but the sting of being turned down by that particular group never completely went away. Now you are careful not to put yourself in a position where you might be rejected, even to the extent of rejecting others before they can reject you.

Fear of Abandonment

Fear of abandonment is very common. Some people know exactly why they suffer from this fear because they remember sitting alone in a darkening apartment the day their father packed his suitcase and left, or the afternoon their mother forgot to pick them up after school and went missing for two days. For others, the root of their fear goes further back, to a time when they used to lie in their crib alone and cry for hours until they fell asleep from exhaustion. These memories, formed before the baby could even walk or talk, may now be hidden behind years of other memories, but they have not lost their potency and their ability to wreak havoc with current relationships.

Fear of Betrayal

Fear of betrayal focuses on disloyalty, duplicity, and treachery. When trust is broken, we lose faith in another's credibility. Then it is understandable that we are anxious, suspicious, and guarded. However, being hypervigilant can have a chilling effect on your relationships.

Fear of Neglect

Fear of neglect is a pervasive reminder of being unloved, unprotected, and undernourished. Being neglected as a child is a terrifying experience that can leave lifelong emotional scars. If you suffered the humiliation of being ignored or treated as if you did not exist, you were the target of neglect. If you were ill or in dire straits and the people you relied on were not there for you, you were neglected. You may have formed alternative alliances to get the support you needed.

Family Legacies

For better or worse, we are all interdependent on one another, and we need our loved ones for the appreciation and support that they can give us. However, our closest relationships become encumbered with conflicted issues when we assume that the way we were brought up *should* be the standard for others. Satisfying relationships don't work that way.

Family legacies are influenced by many factors, including innate biology, cultural heritage, socioeconomic background, brothers and sisters, our unique personality traits, and how we were reared. All these factors will inevitably set the stage for how we are likely to address our conflicts. Examining family legacies gives us a clearer perspective on when, where, and how our close relationships became so difficult to manage.

The four types of family legacies are inner conflict, modeling, guilt, and poor self-esteem. In establishing these, I drew in part on Erik H. Erikson's *Childhood and Society* for his groundbreaking wisdom in the fields of psychoanalysis and human development. Erikson depicted the Eight Ages of Man that reflect the essential inner conflicts associated with each age of growth, as well as our most enduring strengths associated with each stage:

1. Basic trust versus basic mistrust: drive and *hope*
2. Autonomy versus shame and doubt: self-control and *willpower*
3. Initiative versus guilt: direction and *purpose*
4. Industry versus inferiority: method and *competence*

5. Identity versus role confusion: devotion and *fidelity*
6. Intimacy versus isolation: affiliation and *love*
7. Generativity versus stagnation: production and *care*
8. Ego integrity versus despair: renunciation and *wisdom*

Our challenge is to use our energies to persevere and thrive, despite the conflicted predicaments that are bound to occur at any age.[3]

The Family Legacy of Inner Conflict

Even though we hate conflict, the awful truth is that we all have inescapable inner conflicts, which in turn cause conflicts with the people closest to us. Our basic inner conflict, which raises its head at different stages in our lives, is the push–pull between our desire to be independent and to find our own path and our need to be close to our family and loved ones. The conflicts that result from these opposing needs are universal and unavoidable.

Part of the task of becoming your authentic self begins in early life and continues as an ever-evolving process well into adulthood. While you are forging your distinctive personality, you have an inborn drive to individuate, and what you become might be different from what others think you should be.

The family legacy of inner conflict occurs in three stages:

1. In childhood between eighteen and thirty months of age
2. In adolescence from thirteen to twenty-five years of age
3. In midlife from approximately thirty-five to fifty years of age

The First Stage of Inner Conflict. This occurred when you were a young child and had a compulsion to break out of your symbiotic relationship with your parents or other caregivers and to discover what your world was all about. This is when your intense desire to explore went into high gear. As a toddler, you were caught in a bind. You wanted to spread your wings and be independent, but you were thwarted by being wholly dependent on your parents for your essential needs. As a young child, you were trapped in inner conflict—you felt pushed to separate from your parents yet pulled to stay attached to your parents. As a tot, you became contrary and obstinate, and, much to your parents' consternation, your favorite word was *no*. Here you were, this little kid, determined to assert yourself and be your authentic self, even if it meant being unreasonable. It is this same positive energy that motivates you to continue to grow and make beneficial changes as you continue to mature.

The Second Stage of Inner Conflict. When you were a teenager, you predictably exhibited a pattern similar to that of two-year-olds. You felt a push to be independent and to grow up, preferably as fast as possible, and a pull to be dependent, as your parental guidance was still vitally important. Once again, like a tot, you became contrary, defiant, and prone to rebel against parental authority. When it came to doing chores, perhaps you remember saying, "Mom, I can't clean up the kitchen right now. Jimmy and the guys are waiting for me. Sorry, maybe later," and out the door you went. Your parents were probably expecting a minimum of cooperation—"Sure, Dad, I'll be glad to help out"— but that doesn't happen often enough to suit most parents. At this second stage of inner conflict, teens form close attachments to one or more groups of friends and prefer being with them instead of spending leisure time with their parents—ugh!

Many young adults toss caution to the winds, despite repeated parental warnings, and blithely take absurd risks. Teens are usually quite insecure, determined to follow the crowd and do what their friends do, including experiment with illegal substances, steal tires, break windows, become pregnant, and get in a lot of trouble. This is when adolescent hormones are raging. Inner conflict is the name of the game as teenagers are tempted to "go all the way." Boys brag about their prowess with girls, and the developing young women are devastated when their puppy love relationships break up. In her book *My Teenager Is Driving Me Crazy*, teen expert Joyce L. Vedral, Ph.D., explains this dilemma:

> Another reason a teen may defy her parents is to enjoy the pleasure of the moment. . . . In most cases teens hope they won't get caught, even if they know they will. . . . They commit the forbidden act anyway, anticipating the consequences later. Teens often believe that your [parents'] limits are unwarranted, unnecessary, and overcautious. Since they realize through past experience that there's no use in trying to convince you [parents] to change your mind, they take a chance and do it anyway, believing that no harm will be done.[4]

When parent-teen communication and discipline fall through the cracks, high conflict prevails and parent-teen relationships deteriorate. I've noticed that some adults stay contrary and never grow beyond the adolescent stage.

The Third Stage of Inner Conflict. This stage is a decisive one for adults in the throes of a midlife identity crisis. Here again, the push for independence and pull for dependence are reenacted, but with a different twist. As midlifers tackle their demons and pursue their struggles to individuate, they are haunted by uncertainty, ambivalence, indecision, and lack of direction. The midlife crisis has much to do with redefining "me," and this is a highly demanding and difficult transformation.

This excerpt from my book *Should I Stay or Go?* explains the midlife dilemma:

Your midlife inquiry may parallel that of a rebellious teenager as you struggle to be your own person. At once you are
beset with questions: Who am I? What do I want? Where
am I going? You have a compelling urge to be different, to
feel competent, to be important and of value in the scheme
of things. You feel split apart, consumed with an urge to put
aside the old in favor of the new.[5]

At this stage, people tend to make significant changes, such as
entering into a second or third marriage, making a career change,
getting a college degree, moving to a distant location, taking early
retirement, changing their lifestyle, or deciding on a marital sepa-
ration or perhaps an inevitable divorce. Both inner and outer conflicts accompany these events. The need for expert guidance and
direction is often imperative. Some people seek counseling, coaching, and/or mediation to help reduce the stress of life transitions.

The Family Legacy of Modeling

Parents, teachers, and other authority figures all model different
kinds of behavior, and all these influences affect how we develop
our unique personality. We listen to their best teachings, but we
also unconsciously absorb their worst attitudes and behaviors
as well.

Children instinctively imitate the ways parents, teachers, and
others handle their conflicts. As a little kid, you observed optimism and pessimism, kindness and cruelty, cooperation and retaliation, faultfinding and forgiveness, abiding love and contempt. Do
not underestimate the imprint these early examples of conflict left
on your psyche. As a youngster growing up, you copied how your
father and mother handled their conflicts. Resorting to a pattern
that was already familiar, you imitated some of the conduct you
most despised in your parents' ways of relating to each other. You
also exhibited some of their admirable qualities.

The "Peas" Story of Modeling. My earliest memory of having a conflict with my mother was when I was in my terrible twos and sitting in my high chair. I was a skinny, sickly kid, and my mother kept pestering me to eat my peas. I just sat there; I didn't like peas, and I stubbornly refused to eat them. I was testing my mother, and it was her will against mine. Eventually, she gave up and stopped nagging me, and it wasn't until I was in my late teens that I developed an appetite for peas.

That might have been the end of the story, except that I became a mother myself one day. Ironically, I did my best to force my three-year-old daughter, Holly, to eat her peas. She didn't like them either, yet here I was, reenacting the same conflicted drama. I knew full well that peas weren't her favorite veggie, and as you might expect, Holly balked and complained, just as I had done at hear age. What on earth would make me repeat the same scenario? Evidently, I did it by rote; I didn't know any better.

Often family advice runs smack into the family legacy of modeling. This is the origin of the phrase "Do as I say, not as I do!" You probably weren't aware when you were a teen that your parents gave you unspoken permission to act as they did, despite their reprimands to the contrary. Your dad might have warned you not to have sex until you were eighteen, but your mom was only seventeen when you were born. Or your dad might have advised you not to smoke, but he still smokes. These mixed messages are the culprit behind much conflict and confusion. Children are naturally confused when they have contradictory role models to emulate.

Modeling Conflict Styles. In the next chapter, I discuss the five conflict styles that I have identified: the Conflict Avoider, Conflict Fixer, Conflict Goof-Up, Conflict Antagonist, and Conflict Innovator. Conflict styles can be handed down from generation to generation. While we are growing up, we are impressionable, and we automatically absorb our parents' modes of relating. We don't make a conscious decision to match our parents' or grandparents' conflict styles, we just do it without thinking about it.

If your household was noisy and upsetting with lots of arguments and uproar going on, you might have been distressed, or you might have thought that it was no big deal because that's what grown-ups do when they aren't getting along. Because you were exposed to your parents' constant bickering, you are now vulnerable to unthinkingly falling into the same behavior with your partner because it feels normal.

On the other hand, your parents may have sheltered you from their disagreements. If you were raised in a home that was quiet as a tomb, you thought that was normal because you hadn't seen or heard any strife. As far as you knew, dissension happened in the schoolyard but not at home. If silence was the family rule, you didn't bother to ask your parents questions because it seemed like a waste of time. It might not have bothered you if family conversations were pretty much limited to "Yes," "No," "OK," and "Sure." You just tagged along and did what you were told to do because you didn't want to provoke your mom and dad—unless you were so desperate to get their attention that you provoked them anyway.

If you never saw your parents argue, you never learned how to express and resolve your own issues. In that case, when you have a disagreement, you may do what you learned to do best: nothing. In her book *Patterns of Infidelity and Their Treatment*, Emily Brown, marriage and family therapist, addresses the problems with mirroring this dynamic as an adult:

> Communication is limited by the efforts to avoid conflict and also by the couple's collusive focus on idealistic goals instead of on reality. . . . Those who were taught as a child that anger was bad, who were instructed to "look at the positive side of things," or were punished for disagreeing, are

likely to have a hard time expressing dissatisfactions. They also find it difficult to discuss problems. Sometimes they are not even aware of how dissatisfied they are.[6]

If you were lucky, you were reared in a loving, harmonious home, and your parents were able to discuss their differences in a mature manner that did not threaten your sense of security. You knew they were having a disagreement, but they did not fight so long and hard and furiously that you wondered if they even cared about each other. If your parents were able to calmly articulate their disputes and reach some kind of compromise or mutual understanding, you hit the modeling jackpot.

Modeling Polite Behavior. Conflicted relationships flounder on the trash heap when you do not mind your manners. Obviously, parents are our first teachers, and it is their responsibility to teach their children to be polite and respectful. However, fostering a moral compass requires more than teaching children to say, "Please" and "Thank you." Teaching children at an early age to be empathetic is imperative. You do not teach your child anything useful if you say, "You were a bad girl for hitting your sister. I don't want to look at you. Go to your room, and I don't want to hear a peep out of you!" On the other hand, asking children, "How would you feel if your sister pounded on you and really hurt you?" gives youngsters time to think about what they are doing, and that helps them develop a moral compass.

The Family Legacy of Guilt

Parents often feel guilty because they are not convinced they are doing enough to protect their children. At the same time, they worry that they may be doing too much, making their children's lives too easy. You can tell parents are conflicted if they apologize when it is not necessary or refuse to apologize when it would be wise to do so. Guilt is an uncomfortable nagging presence that asks questions and demands answers. Parents wonder:

- "Was I to blame?"
- "What did I do wrong?"
- "Was I justified, or did I overreact?"
- "Was I supposed to apologize?"

When parents are too harsh with their children, there is trouble ahead, but if they are too lenient, there is hell to pay. Many parents feel guilty, knowing that they have neglected their children and denied them consistent nurturing and quality time together, such as taking them to church, helping them learn how to manage their money or how to cook, and teaching them how to behave respect-fully in public. Personally, in regard to child rearing, I believe young adults are seriously deprived if, by the age of sixteen, they have not received from their parents a dignified, ethical under-standing of what appropriate conduct involves.

The legacy of guilt heaps immeasurable conflict on parents and caregivers. Children grow up conflicted because it is second nature for parents to heap guilt trips on them. Kids are told, "Pick up your toys, get off that ladder, don't hit your sister, clean up your room, hang up your clothes, do the dishes, take off your dirty boots," and on and on. These are reasonable requests, but in all likelihood the children will ignore their parents' demands, pretending they didn't hear them or promising to take care of things later. When kids are insubordinate, parents often feel forced to nag. If that doesn't work, they resort to making threats, such as, "No allow-ance for you this week!" or "Do you want to be grounded?" This might get the kids to comply with their parents' demands, but there is a risk that both sides will up the ante. If the child contin-ues to be uncooperative, the parent makes bigger threats, and the conflict escalates. Children feel guilty when parents disapprove of their behavior; the kids feel insecure, not sure they are loved and respected.

There is more to guilt than might be expected. Guilt makes us feel uncomfortable, but it has both productive and unproductive sides.

The Productive Side of Guilt. Where there is possible wrong-doing, guilt creates feelings of humiliation and shame. However, a tad of guilt can motivate you to rethink how you handle your conflicted differences. When you treat your guilt with respect, you pause and rethink how you plan to handle your relationships in a manner that does the least harm possible to all parties. Guilt awakens our conscience, taps into our intuition, and urges us to say, "I'm sorry," and to make amends. Whether or not guilt is justified is determined by each individual's perspective, but I highly recommend that you pay close attention to your guilt, trust your hunches, stop being defensive, and admit when you have made an error in judgment or behavior. Stop kicking yourself, make friends with guilt, and tread lightly when relationships clash. There is much merit when your guilt awakens your conscience, urging you to recognize errors in judgment or behavior and encouraging you to learn how to safely restore harmony and peace.

The Unproductive Side of Guilt. When you persistently embrace an overdeveloped sense of obligation about taking care of others, even when they are not helpless, you experience the destructive side of guilt. You might feel nagging guilt when you are convinced you haven't done enough to please or help your loved ones, even though you have done your very best to achieve this worthy goal. You may assume others are right when they blame you, even though in your heart you know they are being unreasonable. When this happens, you are wallowing in guilt and do not realize you have been brainwashed. In an abusive relationship, you may never feel you have done enough. Remember that your primary obligation is to take care of yourself.

The Family Legacy of Poor Self-Esteem

When children are told by their parents that they are bad and worthless, they often carry these negative scripts as burdensome baggage that clings to them like their skin. For example, the child hears from parents or other authority figures:

- "Why don't you get lost?"
- "I never wanted you in the first place!"
- "You are more trouble than you're worth."
- "You'll never amount to anything."

Character debasement like this convinces youngsters that they are worthless and can't do anything right. As adults, their early script reminds them time and again that others see them as stupid, so they play the part, acting like a dummy.

When you don't believe that you are worthwhile, you betray yourself. You may lose your direction, become unsure of your values, and have fuzzy goals because your creative endeavors are a wish and not a reality. You must believe in yourself in order to love yourself. In his book *The 7 Habits of Highly Effective People*, Stephen R. Covey gives us a reality check on the basics of love:

> If our feelings control our actions, it is because we have abdicated our responsibility and empowered them to do so. . . . Proactive people make *love* a verb. Love is something you do: the sacrifices you make, the giving of self. . . . Love is a value that is actualized through loving actions. Proactive people subordinate feelings to values. Love, the feeling, can be recaptured.[7]

We live in a restless world where many of us feel shortchanged. We want more, but we don't believe we are lovable, valuable, and worthy. Youngsters feel cheated if they don't get their parents' love and approval. Children develop low self-esteem when they don't get the recognition they deserve. So many of us have strengths and talents that are not fulfilled.

Paradoxically, as we copy our parents' mistakes, many of us have the audacity to blame our parents because we didn't turn out to be perfect gems. It's not unusual for grown-ups to overreact like two- and three-year-old kids, kicking and screaming because Mommy was mean and Daddy left home. We are magnanimous when we forgive our parents because they didn't know how to responsibly resolve their differences. Let's be gracious enough to appreciate our parents for teaching us as much as they did.

Let's not forget that acts of commission or omission are opportunities for us. They are enough to motivate us to learn better ways to handle our hassles. If you saw your mother crying frantically while your father was too scared to speak up, or if you heard your parents arguing into the wee hours of the night, regard these experiences as a lesson in the importance of speaking politely, without alienating your loved ones. In a conversation, Rabbi Ronald M. Shapiro of Milwaukee, Wisconsin, wisely told me, "Truly, what makes a person spiritual is how we interact honestly and openly with others, without feeling the need to coerce them to bend to our position and convictions."

Questions for Reflection

- Did you feel safe and comfortable when you were growing up?
- Were family members frigid and distant or considerate and friendly?
- Do you recall tiptoeing around, too scared to open your mouth for fear of upsetting your parents or grandparents?
- Are you crippled by feelings of fear and anger?
- Do you remember any early traumatic experiences that might have left a blemish on your relationships today?
- Are you a risk taker, or do you prefer to play it safe when you are involved in disputes with loved ones, friends, or coworkers?
- Do you notice when you are modeling another person's behavior?
- Has modeling the conduct of others been a positive or negative experience for you?
- Has humiliation been a major or minor factor when you clash with others?
- Do you ever demonstrate that you care about your loved ones?

Journaling

As you answer the preceding touchy questions, you are addressing specific aspects of your family of origin. Describe in writing how you related to your parents, siblings, grandparents, and teachers when you were growing up, and write about what you learned about conflict as a child that has left a lasting impression on you. Discuss in your journal how your fear and anger warns you not to tackle a grizzly bear, but you take a risk and do it anyway. Or if you try to avoid conflict at all costs, write about your feelings of guilt, shame, and regret when your relationships get toxic. This is sensitive work to do, so be patient. You are in the process of learning to perceive conflict in many different ways.

4

The Five Conflict Styles

After years of study, reflection, and experience with many hundreds of clients—not to mention decades of my own life experience—I have determined that there are five conflict styles: Conflict Avoider, Conflict Fixer, Conflict Goof-Up, Conflict Antagonist, and Conflict Innovator. As you identify with one or more of the five conflict styles, you will learn many strategies that show you how to relate to your loved ones without being defensive.

As you reflect on the following descriptions of the five conflict styles, see if you recognize yourself in one or more of them. You may use one approach quite consistently, or you may have a primary style and a secondary style. It is not unusual to switch gears for different settings or with different people. Perhaps you are a Conflict Innovator and are able to hold your temper with everyone on earth—except your mother-in-law! Maybe you are a Conflict Antagonist who does not hesitate to raise a ruckus at home but intuitively recognizes that a combative style is not appreciated in the workplace.

You and your partner's style(s) may not always be the same. Depending on your personality, disposition, and circumstances as well as how you communicate, you may abruptly adopt an alternate style, from humane words of comfort to thoughtless words of contempt. Each conflict style has unique dimensions that determine how you will interact as a couple. As you identify with one or more of these styles, growing together is likely to take on a whole new meaning.

Each of the conflict styles has both positive and negative characteristics, except the Conflict Innovator, which is a practical approach. If you can identify the conflict style of others in your life, you will have a better understanding of the way they handle disputes, which will help you with your difficult conversations.

Conflict Avoiders

When I was nine years old, I had a brief conversation with my mother that had a profound impact on me because it came so unexpectedly. My mother casually said, "Aunt Tillie and I have been talking about you, and she thinks you are afraid of me." My mother paused briefly and then bluntly asked, "Are you afraid of me?"

This was a terribly awkward moment in my young life. I understood that my mother would never have dared to ask such a risky question without my Aunt Tillie's nudging. I was trapped if I told the truth—that I really was afraid of her. In a flash, I had terrifying fantasies of grueling interrogations about why I was so scared of my mother. My head was abuzz as I conjured up all kinds of horrible thoughts of hurting my mother's feelings because I was critical of her.

Then I got confused because I kept hearing my mother's message, "If you haven't anything good to say about anyone, don't say it." Now for sure I was in a bind. As I look back, how could a naive, introverted, frightened kid answer such a challenging question? What would I say? How would I defend myself? Would I blame my mother? All I could think of was misery for my mother and torture for me. I hated the thought of being on trial with a verdict of guilty!

Honestly, I loved my parents and I knew they loved me, so I gave her my next best answer, "No, Mother, I'm not afraid of you!" I knew I was telling a little white lie, but first and foremost I was a peacekeeper. I habitually kept a low profile, I kept my thoughts to myself, and I rarely made a fuss. The notion of purposefully upsetting either of my parents was not on my radar screen. Frankly, I couldn't bear the thought of anyone being angry with me.

At such a young age, my purpose in life was to preserve calm and ward off any controversy, even though that was impossible. I was a pleaser then, and I still try to please others whenever possible. In truth, I lied to save myself, and I lied to save my mother's feelings because I didn't want to create a scene that I knew I couldn't handle. I was grateful my mother never asked this question again. As for my little white lie—that I'll never forget!

Conflict Avoiders: "I Don't Want to Talk About It!"

As a rule, Conflict Avoiders are too intimidated to confront anyone. The very thought of it gets them befuddled with all kinds of extraneous stuff, so they change the subject or walk away and say nothing. The following comments indicate why Conflict Avoiders don't confront others, even when they are feeling angry:

- He said, "For me, confrontation is like taking cod-liver oil, so I try to be tactful."
- She said, "I'm mousy and too timid to confront anyone. My mother was mousy, too, so I guess I learned that trait from her."
- He said, "When I finally work up the nerve to confront her, she bites my head off. I'm not stupid, but I don't know what to say to her."
- She said, "I'm such a wimp, I'm afraid to confront him. I know I'll cry and make a fool of myself."

- He said, "Confrontation is my nemesis. I'm a lousy communicator."
- She said, "He gives me a dirty look and I shrivel up. I don't know if I'll ever have the nerve to confront him."
- She said, "When we bicker about little things, he raises the stakes and I get scared."
- He said, "I know my relationship would improve with her if I knew the right way to bring up these problems. Then maybe she would understand me better."

Conflict Avoiders are not trying to be invisible; they just want a tranquil life. Their goal is to be spared any kind of commotion or verbal assault. Like most people, they are hungry for recognition of their accomplishments, and they thrive on praise and encouragement. Conflict Avoiders prefer a well-ordered, harmonious environment, and when there is strife, they protect themselves with their avoidant repertoire, which includes:

- Denial ("Everything is great!")
- Minimizing ("It's not that big a deal.")
- Condoning ("It's fine, really.")
- Enduring ("I can live with it.")
- Ignoring ("What problem?")
- Appeasing ("Whatever you want, Dear.")

Conflict Avoiders will tell you up front, "I'm not going to ruffle any feathers." They prize their independence, value their quiet time, and prefer to stay calm and serene. Conflict Avoiders play it safe because they detest the way disagreements disturb their equilibrium, and they usually sweep a lot of problems under the rug. They don't like feeling awkward and distressed. They tend to minimize what others perceive as friction and often say yes when they mean no. Conflict Avoiders pretend their conflicts will go away and hope their relationships will magically get easier.

Conflict Avoiders rarely argue when relationships are contentious. With a poker face, they would rather give in and stuff their anger. They cringe when loved ones are annoyed with them. They are so intimidated and afraid that inside they are thinking, "I don't want to make you mad at me; that's the last thing I need!" But they are too timid to say these words aloud to others. In the book *Crucial Conversations*, the authors clarify the thought process of Conflict Avoiders:

> Sometimes we choose personal safety over dialogue. Rather than add to the pool of meaning, and possibly make waves along the way, we go to silence. We're so uncomfortable with the immediate conflict that we accept the *certainty* of bad results to avoid the *possibility* of uncomfortable conversation. We choose (at least in our minds) peace over conflict.[1]

To justify their silence, Conflict Avoiders use rationalizations like the following:

- "I don't want to make a fuss. It's not worth it."
- "I don't want to tell her. It would hurt her feelings if she knew."
- "There's too much going on right now, so it's best if I just let it go."
- "I haven't got time for all this Mickey Mouse conflicted stuff."

Instead of talking about what's eating at them, Conflict Avoiders fantasize about running away. Rather than engage in a dispute, they will walk out the back door or roll over and turn out the light. Some Conflict Avoiders can be found in gyms or at bars after work, gathering the courage to go home. In general, women are quick to see the consequences of living with a Conflict Avoider. Women tend to initiate discussions more than men, who are more likely to tune out what they are hearing or to forget what they've been told. If you put all Conflict Avoiders in a room together, there would be more men than women. If this surprises you, think about the stereotypical image of Dad behind the newspaper.

Because controversy is off-limits, Conflict Avoiders have been suffering in silence since early childhood. Trouble brews when Conflict Avoiders get annoyed time and again, as they are prone to be passive, suppress their hurt feelings, hold a grudge, and let their resentment simmer on the back burner. When Conflict Avoiders are repeatedly offended, they do a slow burn. Over time, their resentments get out of hand, and much to their dismay, they find they are in the throes of a toxic love-hate relationship. Regrettably, Conflict Avoiders feel helpless to do anything to restore order because they haven't a clue how to repair their damaged relations. It is common for Conflict Avoiders to feel distraught yet lack the insight they need to handle their upsetting circumstances.

Conflict Avoiders

Their motto: "I don't want to talk about it!"

What they assume: If they don't discuss their conflicts, the conflicts will go away.

Their intention: To keep the peace at any price.

The costs of being a Conflict Avoider: Feeling frustrated, resentful, and disillusioned.

The benefits of being a Conflict Avoider: Turmoil does not get out of hand.

As a lifelong method of operation, avoiding conflict simply does not work. It is important for our human dignity to set limits on what we will and will not tolerate. Disagreements are an inevitable part of life, and when we fail to work through them, we limit the scope of our experiences.

Negative Habits of Conflict Avoiders

Conflict Avoiders are afraid to draw the line regarding the bad behavior of others. When they "hush up and put up," it has the effect of giving others permission to be snide, disrespectful, and malicious. They are willing to put up with discontent indefinitely, but over time, they are at risk of fueling the fires of conflict. They also diminish their power by staying silent for so long. Conflict Avoiders are given to errors of omission because they find it so much easier to back off when there are disputes. Their coping mechanism is to build emotional walls to insulate themselves from suffering.

Positive Habits of Conflict Avoiders

Conflict Avoiders are peacemakers at heart. They strive to make their relationships as harmonious and friendly as possible; they are pleasers who are ever ready at their loved one's beck and call. They are generally patient and tolerant and willing to compromise. They might be churning inside, but they refuse to stir up more trouble by escalating potential clashes. In order to keep their relationships on an even keel, Conflict Avoiders back off, accepting the status quo and/or letting time work on their behalf.

Conflict Avoiders are not drama queens. They refuse to incite needless conflict. They stay in control of their baser emotions and have a great deal of experience in holding their hostile feelings in check.

Ted's Story

My client Ted is a classic Conflict Avoider. He tried to avoid last night's argument with his wife, Sara, by saying, "I don't want to talk about it," but she kept pestering him, and he got sucked into quarreling once again. Ted is at his wit's end. He tries to please Sara, but she nags and criticizes him, and when he tries to object to her demands, a futile argument usually ensues. Ted's preference is to let Sara rant and rave and hopefully blow off some steam, but when he says nothing, Sara bitterly complains that he will not communicate with her.

Ted is a nervous wreck. He has been having trouble concentrating at work. All he can think about is his derailed marriage, and he doesn't know how to get his conflicted relationship problems resolved.

Conflict Avoider Quiz: Questions to Ask Yourself

Use the following questions to decide whether you are, or are not, a Conflict Avoider:

1. Do you prefer to keep the peace at all costs?
2. Do you find yourself saying things like, "Why won't he just get off my back?" or, "This isn't fair—I need my space!"
3. When someone locks horns with you, do you find ways to disappear?
4. Do other people in your life tell you that you are in denial or try unsuccessfully to engage you in conversations about difficult matters?
5. Do you perceive yourself as having little power to influence others?

Journaling

As you reflect upon the preceding questions, write about your most satisfying experiences as a Conflict Avoider relating to another Conflict Avoider. If most of your interactions have been with people who have a different conflict style than yours, then contrast the way you relate to them and how they interact with you. Focus on how you and the other person converse when a controversial issue arises. Note your attitude and the other person's frame of mind. Write about your intention and the actual outcome of your conversations. Did some issues get lost? Were your ideas addressed? Were you polite? Was it difficult to communicate because either you or the other person shut down? Be specific as you write about what you enjoy about being a Conflict Avoider. Then write about your frustrations with being a Conflict Avoider.

Conflict Fixers

The second style is for those people who want to fix conflicts—both their own and those of other people. The problem is that they don't always know the right way to do it!

Conflict Fixers: "Honey, I'm Only Trying to Help You!"

Conflict Fixers embrace disagreements because turmoil provides them with an opportunity to save the day. Their mission in life is to protect their loved ones and to make their close relationships as perfect as possible. In fact, it drives them crazy to let conflicts fester for an hour, a day, or, heaven forbid, indefinitely. Conflict Fixers strive to have a good marriage and gratifying relationships with others. They are eager to discuss problems and like to have conflicts resolved in a hurry.

Conflict Fixers take pride in being a helpmate. They are conscientious, meticulous, and benevolent. Conflict Fixers strive to have a good marriage, are eager to discuss problems, and like to have conflict resolved before it has an opportunity to worsen.

Because they are eager to help, Conflict Fixers are advice givers. Their intentions are honorable, so you might think they would always be welcome, but such is not the case, because their manner of trying to fix relationships is often flawed. They assume they know what's best, but they may be wrong. In their efforts to help others improve their relationship skills, they can do considerable harm.

Conflict Fixers are given to lecturing and criticizing their loved ones. When they are whiney and negative, their attitude is counterproductive, as they are not likely to be aware that their lecturing aggravates others. Their superior attitude makes others feel inferior and unworthy. Thus Conflict Fixers are sorely disappointed when their supposedly sage advice is blatantly ignored.

Conflict Fixers hate to be censured, but they dish out plenty of their own complaints. Their pride prevents them from admitting their mistakes, and, like many people, they hope to hide their failures. Sometimes they presume that their nosy interference in other people's lives is permissible, but it doesn't take long before they discover that such outreach is not appreciated.

The profile of Conflict Fixers is extensive, ranging from finicky-fussy types who complain if a pin is out of place, to know-it-all rescuers, to intelligent folk who have a vast fund of information at their disposal. Conflict Fixers can be impatient, pushy, and critical, or they can be modest heroes or heroines with ingenious answers that make life better for others.

I have observed that more women than men earnestly believe they were born to be Conflict Fixers whose mission in life is to fix other people's troubles. If wishing were so, this would be true, but "fixing" oneself is a person's personal task to do.

Conflict Fixers are well-meaning advice givers who are happy to give their loved ones accurate information and sensible answers. They take pride in being supportive, encouraging, and accommodating with their close associates. They enjoy cooperative ventures and are proud of accomplishing worthy goals. A Conflict Fixer's greatest joy is to be vindicated and held blameless, so they can smugly say, "You see, I told you so!"

Conflict Fixers

Their motto: "Honey, I'm only trying to help you!"

What they assume: They are great problem solvers because conflict resolution should be easy.

Their intention: To offer you their sage advice and solve your problems.

The costs of being a Conflict Fixer: Being overbearing and insensitive without realizing it.

The benefits of being a Conflict Fixer: The desire to fix conflicts before they get worse.

Negative Habits of Conflict Fixers

Conflict Fixers make the assumption that they know what is best for their mate, their significant other, their parents, or their close friends. Unfortunately, their manner of trying to fix other people's relationships is frequently flawed. When Conflict Fixers are frustrated and unable to fix their own difficult relationships, they often morph into the Conflict Antagonist style (discussed later in this chapter). Then turmoil prevails!

Positive Habits of Conflict Fixers

Conflict Fixers want to make everything better. They like to think of themselves as masters of logic as they proudly show off their reasoning abilities. To their credit, they are generally verbally expressive and eager to tackle contentious issues as quickly as possible. Conflict Fixers are smart, knowledgeable, and famous for giving sound advice when it is sought out. Provided their wise counsel and advice has been requested, their creative ideas are welcome.

Conflict Fixer Quiz: Questions to Ask Yourself

Use the following questions to decide whether or not you are a Conflict Fixer:

1. When there is a dispute, do you want to make everything better?
2. Do you find it easy or difficult to find solutions for disputes?
3. Are you satisfied with how you handle your own clashes?
4. Have you ever been told by someone to butt out or get lost when you were only trying to help them with a conflict?
5. Have you had any successful experiences being a Conflict Fixer with your spouse, partner, family members, workplace colleagues, and/or friends?

George's Story

My client George is a frustrated Conflict Fixer. When he is annoyed with Helen, it is hard for him to feel loving toward her. He wishes she would be more independent and not so clingy and needy. It seemed clear to George that there were a few things Helen could do to enrich her life. He suggested she take computer classes, get a better job, redo her hair, and fix herself up. She burst into tears. George said, "Helen, I'm only telling you this for your own good." Helen went to spend the night at her mother's. George went to the tavern to have a few drinks.

Journaling

As you answer the questions in the "Conflict Fixer Quiz," write about your successes and failures on those occasions when you have been a Conflict Fixer. Note if you see a predictable pattern—for example, you have a lot of patience and the other person is short on patience, or vice versa. Write about any contrasting points of view that have gotten you and another person mad at each other. Describe your feelings and what worries you the most when you are poles apart because you disagree with someone.

Conflict Goof-Ups

Like Conflict Fixers, Conflict Goof-Ups mean well and care about their loved ones. However, like Conflict Avoiders, they are too insecure to risk confrontation. They have many anxious moments because controversy has them stymied.

Conflict Goof-Ups: "Whatever I Say, It's Not Good Enough!"

When Conflict Goof-Ups speak with the people who matter the most to them, they often stutter and stammer. Much to their consternation, they are ineffective communicators. At their best, they have foot-in-mouth disease that causes great confusion. At their worst, they will deliberately lie and manipulate.

Conflict Goof-Ups speak in vague terms and tend to irritate the very people they hope to impress the most. They yearn to communicate with ease, but instead their words come out garbled and sometimes incoherent. Conflict Goof-Ups aren't prepared to have sensible conversations with their loved ones. Instead they keep their relationships in a dither with awkward, stupid conversations.

Some Conflict Goof-Ups are Life Goof-Ups. In their nervous, distracted state, they trigger more layers of conflict. They carelessly procrastinate and don't complete the tasks they promised to do. They are likely to be forgetful and lose track of time. They tend to be irresponsible and unreliable and will say yes when they mean no. They don't like to be pinned down. They don't like being pressured to explain what, when, how, or why they forgot the keys or didn't remember to order the fruit basket. They annoy their loved ones with flimsy excuses. Conflict Goof-Ups find it easier to fib than to tell the truth. When they have been deceitful, they try to cover up their tracks with turmoil. In turn, they find themselves in the thicket of personal and interpersonal conflict that is exhausting for all concerned. No wonder they are plagued with fears of being inadequate.

Conflict Goof-Ups are so insecure that they protect their fragile ego by being sneaky. As defensive manipulators, they don't tell the truth and will lie to cover up their inadequacies. Some Conflict Goof-Ups withhold vital information that their partner, parents, supervisor, or friends need to know. Ultimately, trust is destroyed when the missing information is finally revealed under considerable duress.

Conflict Goof-Ups have an uncanny knack for getting others mad at them. This has the effect of throwing a smokescreen around the real issues. Anticipating the worst will happen, they keep their close relationships off balance.

Conflict Goof-Ups sabotage intelligent dialogue in several ways:

- They get defensive, which makes it hard to talk to them in a reasonable manner.
- They can be passive-aggressive, meaning they behave in an insincere way by hiding their mean streak under phony congeniality.
- They maneuver the conversation by changing the subject to distract the other person.
- They tell outright lies to throw a wrench in the conversation.
- They play stupid by asking irrelevant questions that insult the other person's intelligence.

Tongue-tied and awkward, Conflict Goof-Ups cause extensive bashing and blaming. They are in such a fog that they often don't realize how their inadequate communication adds another layer of conflict to their already pressing problems. They tend to get depressed because their thinking is scattered all over the map. In their distraught state of mind, they become easily overwhelmed by controversy.

When Conflict Goof-Ups are put on the spot and pressured to explain what they did wrong or why they said something foolish, they dump their fury on their closest associates. When they are cornered, they will turn around and fault others for demanding answers that are not on the tip of their tongue. In her book *Honor Your Anger: How Transforming Your Anger Style Can Change Your Life*,

Beverly Engel notes that the "initial sense of shame often fosters a subsequent anger—a humiliated fury—as an attempt to provide temporary relief from the debilitating experiences and effects of shame . . . this fury is easily directed toward others."[2]

Conflict Goof-Ups rationalize their own mistakes by finding fault with their loved ones and peers. They fear their own rage and are prone to loathe themselves and damn their adversaries for making their relationships so difficult to manage. After they have made a toxic mess of their close relationships by repeatedly inciting the wrath of their loved ones, Conflict Goof-Ups may do a full retreat by giving everyone the silent treatment or even by becoming completely estranged. Sometimes Conflict Goof-Ups get so confused and defensive that they unwittingly become full-fledged Conflict Antagonists (discussed next), and when that happens their malicious intent can be downright scary.

To the good, Conflict Goof-Ups feel inspired and fulfilled when they are serving those outside their circle of family and friends in protective, wholesome ways. They have the fortitude to patiently help others work out their problems. They can be good listeners. Conflict Goof-Ups often have a big heart, and their energy knows no bounds when it comes to serving those outside their immediate connections. They are often talented members of the helping professions, including counselors, mediators, facilitators, healers, doctors, nurses, and ministers. Some are conscientiously invested in teaching, mentoring, or performing community service. In these settings, they display their strengths and have the fortitude to patiently help others work out their conflicted concerns.

Conflict Goof-Ups assume no one will notice that their antics are keeping their interactions in disarray. They rationalize that somehow their relationships will stabilize. Slowly but surely, Conflict Goof-Ups can learn how to speak up and confront others, thereby enhancing their poor self-esteem. As they gain self-confidence and more insight, they may strengthen and revitalize their closest relationships.

Conflict Goof-Ups

Their motto: "Whatever I say, it's not good enough!"

What they assume: No one will notice their manipulations.

Their intention: To cover up their ineptness.

The costs of being a Conflict Goof-Up: Feeling rejected, victimized, and overwhelmed by conflicted issues.

The benefits of being a Conflict Goof-Up: Capable of being a caring, trustworthy friend.

Negative Habits of Conflict Goof-Ups

Conflict Goof-Ups create chaos to distract others because they don't know how to address their disputes or the disorder they made. When Conflict Goof-Ups feel pressured to explain what went haywire, their anxiety and stress intensifies and they can't think clearly or rationally. This sets up a chain reaction of frustration and futility because they are not sufficiently skilled at dealing with the repercussions of miscommunication, and then they feel utterly discouraged. Often, Conflict Goof-Ups tend to doubt themselves and will devalue their own worth.

Positive Habits of Conflict Goof-Ups

Conflict Goof-Ups have remorse and regret when they don't measure up to their own or another's expectations. They usually will admit they are wrong and apologize profusely for letting other people down. Conflict Goof-Ups are often hungry to improve their communication so they can constructively confront and revitalize their close relationships. Once they are invested in personal growth, they tend to work diligently to improve their conversational skills, as they know full well that it takes time and energy to change oneself.

Elena's Story

Elena is a Conflict Goof-Up. She loves Carmine and tells him so often, but she knows this is not enough to rescue their conflicted marriage. Elena admits she is intimidated by her husband and afraid she cannot measure up to his brainpower. She loathes when he criticizes her in public. To Elena's dismay, she falls apart when she tries to talk to Carmine about their conflicted issues. She says, "I'm like a bumbling idiot. I can't ever say anything right!" Because Elena can't seem to express herself clearly, Carmine discounts what she has to say. Elena actually is making her worst nightmare come true.

Conflict Goof-Up Quiz: Questions to Ask Yourself

Use the following questions to decide whether you are, or are not, a Conflict Goof-Up:

1. Do other people comment on your lack of time-management skills, disorganization, difficulty accomplishing tasks, and trouble getting along?
2. Have you ever lied to someone just to get him or her off your back?
3. How likely are you to blame others when things go wrong?
4. Does it piss you off when others try to pin you down?
5. How do you feel when your back is against the wall?

Journaling

As you reflect on the preceding questions, write about how difficult it is to converse when your back is against the wall. Whether or not you are a Conflict Goof-Up, you have surely had this experience. Write about feeling like a scapegoat or being the favorite kid when you were growing up. Be specific in writing about the disputes that bother you the most. Try to recall occasions when others have manipulated or deliberately misinterpreted you. Then try to remember if you have ever been manipulative or have misinterpreted someone else.

Conflict Antagonists

If you haven't yet found your conflict style, maybe this one is for you. The Conflict Antagonist doesn't mind conflict and is willing to go to great lengths to win the fight, even if it means losing the war.

Conflict Antagonists: "I'm Going to Win This Battle!"

Historically, if your parents argue, if your grandparents argue, if your siblings and the rest of the family argue, you automatically have unspoken permission to argue. You assume that everyone argues, so you do it automatically. You get mad, mad, mad because you are faced with attack, attack, attack, and you aren't thinking about the repercussions of your vicious remarks. Your arguments are a negative way of staying connected, albeit not a prudent way to communicate.

Conflict Antagonists tend to be unpredictable. They are usually charming, deferential, and dignified in the public arena, but there are times when they might take a dislike to a relative or coworker, and then their mean-spirited side comes out. Conflict Antagonists are selective about who they treat politely and who they treat disrespectfully. With their buddies, they are usually affable, cheerful, and fun loving. However, they easily can become agitated with anyone who is living under the same roof with them. Anytime Conflict Antagonists have a disagreement with family members, a friend, or a coworker, they get hotheaded and curt. As a rule, when they are upset, they become argumentative. When two Conflict Antagonists duke it out, hope for respectfully resolving their differences becomes a lost cause. They hurl insults back and forth and are split into enemy camps. After they are thoroughly exhausted, they will take a breather and cool down until another conflict sets them off, and then they are up to their malicious tricks again.

Conflict Antagonists don't hold back. Their self-absorbed, overconfident stance causes them to attack others with virtually no thought of the dire consequences of their aggressive behavior. Because they believe the problem is entirely the other person's doing, they tend to make accusations like:

- "How can you possibly think like that?"
- "You don't know what you are talking about!"
- "Who do you think you are, blasting me like that?"
- "You are so stubborn. Why won't you see it my way?"

Conflict Antagonists have a reputation for being arrogant, egotistical, authoritarian, rigid, and controlling. This is why they have such a difficult time sustaining viable relationships. They frequently seek revenge ("You were mean to me, so I'll strike back at you!"). If anyone dares to stand up to them in an aggressive way, Conflict Antagonists are apt to turn vicious. They tend to intimidate, threaten, coerce, and terrify, thereby trashing any hope for managing couple conflict as their partnership flounders on the brink of disillusionment and despair. They give no thought to the diminishing returns of the energy expended in a fight that goes down the drain and leaves both parties distressed and disgusted. Their once-caring relationship goes south as hope for better treatment wanes.

When Conflict Antagonists go on the warpath, they put a lot of hostile energy into settling the score. Whether the problem is a major or minor disagreement, a bad headache, naughty kids, an upsetting day at work, or a lost briefcase, Conflict Antagonists want others to feel their pain and suffering. They call negative attention to themselves because they are hungry for love, approval, and appreciation. They create a great deal of conflict for nonsensical reasons, such as the need to be all powerful, the urge to create drama, and the desire to feel their issues are the most important. They may continue to battle it out even though they are wrong, just to get the upper hand.

Conflict Antagonists are not always unbearable. When they are on the same page as everyone else, they can be entertaining and

Conflict Antagonists

Their motto: "I'm going to win this battle!"

What they assume: It's my way or the highway.

Their intention: To go on the warpath for sweet revenge.

The costs of being a Conflict Antagonist: Mistaking another person's assertion for aggression.

The benefits of being a Conflict Antagonist: Having the courage of one's convictions.

supportive. With enhanced self-esteem, they may lose the need to browbeat others and learn how to resolve their differences amicably.

Negative Habits of Conflict Antagonists

When Conflict Antagonists are upset with anyone, they believe their temper tantrums are justified. The only person who gets a kick out of arguing with a Conflict Antagonist is another Conflict Antagonist. Everyone else gets a headache from this exercise in futility. Because they don't know how to stop their arguments, Conflict Antagonists secretly live in toxic torment.

Conflict Antagonists see no need to be open-minded or to seek the validity of other points of view. By making ordinary give-and-take difficult, if not impossible, Conflict Antagonists limit the amount of information they actually take in, which puts them at risk of being uninformed.

Positive Habits of Conflict Antagonists

Conflict Antagonists are not subtle. You always know where you stand, although it might be in the corner with a dunce's cap on your head. When Conflict Antagonists learn how to calm down and consistently curtail their cantankerous ways, they can achieve loving, cordial, honest, and respectful relationships. When they mind their manners and show caring concern for their loved ones, their relationships perk up and family members and friends are happier.

In his book *Healing from Family Rifts: Ten Steps to Finding Peace After Being Cut Off from a Family Member*, Mark Sichel describes two sisters, Alice and Lisa. From his description, you can see what it is like to live with a Conflict Antagonist:

"I've always had to walk on eggshells with my sister Lisa," Alice told me. "Ever since I can remember, if Lisa didn't get

her way, there'd be hell to pay . . . the myth she tried to per-
petuate was Lisa knows best. . . . Whenever I've disagreed
with her, it's been taken as a slap in the face rather than a difference of opinion. I mean, she's always been fine if you yes
her to death, even if you don't mean it."[3]

My client Clarisse had a serious mistrust issue with her Conflict
Antagonist father. She explained, "I was always scared of my dad
when I was growing up because he often got into a rage over petty
things, and then he would take it out on me. When he went on a
rampage, he would say, 'I'm going to kill you!' And I was never
sure if he meant it or not. I was always on pins and needles when
he was near me."

Clarisse asked me, "Could that be why I have a hard time trusting other men?" I responded, "Conflict Antagonists can be dan-
gerous when they lose control of their hostile emotions, so it is

Conflict Antagonist Quiz: Questions to Ask Yourself

Use the following questions to decide whether you are, or
are not, a Conflict Antagonist:

1. In general, do you respect others' points of view, or is it
   your way or the highway?
2. How often do you feel entitled to seek revenge?
3. Do arguments and disputes make you feel more or less
   powerful?
4. How often do you have arguments that affect your close
   relationships in a negative manner?
5. When others disagree with you, what is your initial
   reaction?

only natural that your first impulse would be to shy away from guys. But remember, there are decent men out there, so don't give up your dreams."

Journaling

Conflict Antagonists often exhibit, or provoke, angry behavior. Write about your angry emotions, and look inward to find out what it is that scares you the most. Have you tried to sensibly speak up to others? Write about the consequences of these conversations and whether they were satisfactory or detrimental to your relationships. Then write about what you are discovering about this conflict style.

Conflict Innovators

This is the fifth and final conflict style. Conflict Innovators put into practice everything that is *good* about conflict. This style may seem idealized, but it is achievable with good intentions and lots of practice!

Conflict Innovators: "Let's Be Sensible and Consider Our Options"

In his book *Where Have All the Leaders Gone?*, Lee Iacocca identifies the nine Cs of leadership: Curiosity, Creativity, Communicator, Character, Courage, Conviction, Charisma, Competency, and Common Sense.[4] Conflict Innovators are the brave, fearless leaders of this definition. Not only must they be expert problem solvers, but also their integrity demands that they be fair, balanced, and unbiased.

Conflict Innovators understand that being cordial helps their conversations stay on an even keel. They are creative thinkers and are sensible enough to soft-pedal it when they are negotiating with contentious people. They have learned that it is wise to speak respectfully to others, even when they are feeling frustrated and irritated with them.

Conflict Innovators strive to be humble, flexible, and compassionate. When they are out of sorts, they apologize profusely for not being as kind as they should be. When they have used poor judgment, they feel guilty and make amends. Their integrity is a mainstay as they collaborate and negotiate each conflicted issue, one at a time.

Conflict Innovators have learned from experience. Usually they have been burned and learned the hard way, through trial and error, as well as by intuition and insight, how to wisely address their conflicted concerns.

Because achieving trusting relationships is of paramount importance to them, Conflict Innovators are forthright and do their homework. Tactfully and prudently, they present their case and search for a mutually acceptable solution. They are invested in learning the high art of diplomacy. Conflict Innovators have a uniquely constructive approach to disputes:

- They are honest.
- They consider the pros and cons of an impasse.
- They look at the broad picture: what is working versus what is not, what is toxic versus what is valid and worthwhile.
- They plan their discussion and rehearse how they will present their case.
- They make certain they will be able to do whatever they promise to do.

- They do their best to stay calm and not overreact.
- They think before they say anything.
- They speak directly to the other person and clearly state what they want.
- They are willing to suggest a compromise.
- They follow through responsibly on verbal or written agreements.

Conflict Innovators acknowledge the importance of tact, discretion, and diplomacy. They treat others as equals, and each person involved in the discussion shares the leadership role. Conflict Innovators recognize that first they must clean up their own act, and others must fix their conflicted selves, before mutual honesty, respect, and compassion can be a reality. Mutuality plays a major part in their connections with others. Their authenticity paves the way for supportive mutual respect.

Conflict Innovators do their best to step outside their comfort zone. They understand the necessity of stretching, of doing what is uncomfortable, to make their needs known. During their discussions, Conflict Innovators are careful to avoid common traps:

- They are not squirrelly about their intentions, knowing that that makes people nervous.
- They are not defensive.
- They do not argue about who is right and who is wrong.
- They do not allow their strong emotions to get the better of them.

Conflict Innovators are a mix of each conflict style because they are human, just like everyone else.

- When they are tired, they might "avoid" listening carefully because their mind is wandering elsewhere.

- At times, they are impatient, and in their rush to "fix" the problem, they may make incorrect assumptions.
- At times they may "goof up" when they misconstrue what others say.
- Occasionally, they explode because they are infuriated, and then they show an "antagonistic" edge. However, they stop themselves before their anger gets out of hand.

Conflict Innovators know that disagreements beg for compassion and acceptance. They understand that the better part of wisdom suggests that they not put any more energy into trying to be an enabler or a rescuer. They are willing to adapt and change aspects of themselves as needed. In other words, Conflict Innovators acknowledge and accept their limitations! They do their best to maintain an optimistic attitude, pardoning others and themselves by learning that it's possible to defuse most skirmishes before they have a chance to get started.

Conflict Innovators

Their motto: "Let's be sensible and consider our options."

What they assume: The more I learn from my mistakes, the less I have to regret.

Their intention: They pick their battles—the fewer the better.

The costs of being a Conflict Innovator: None.

The benefits of being a Conflict Innovator: They'll confront when necessary, so others will know their limitations.

Conflict Innovators understand the importance of sitting down at the negotiation table and talking common sense. In the event that negotiations reach an impasse for any reason, they will seek the expertise of psychiatrists, psychologists, marriage and family counselors, social workers, life coaches, mediators, ministers, or trusted friends to talk through their logjam in order to be better prepared to settle their clashes in a congenial manner.

In her article "The Road Less Traveled," published in *Psychotherapy Networker*, Marian Sandmaier describes people as finding comfort in the familiar:

> Whether or not we like to admit it, most of us are creatures of habit. We're embedded in our daily routines and familiar surroundings, deriving a kind of quiet security from the choices we've made—about the work we do, about what we deeply believe, about the kind of difference we want to make in our lives. There's a sense of shelter, even sanctuary, in this known world.[5]

While being a Conflict Avoider, Conflict Fixer, Conflict Goof-Up, or Conflict Antagonist may be your familiar bus stop, from now on you have a new and improved destination: Conflict Innovator.

Peggy's Story

Peggy, a Conflict Innovator, said, "When our son Eddie came home with a tattoo, I wanted there to be some consequences. He didn't ask us for permission. He just went with some friends to some tattoo parlor and came home with Chinese lettering on his chest. I needed to talk to Roland about how to handle this situation, because I couldn't handle it alone. Whatever we chose to do, we would have to agree on it together. I was chasing Roland around the kitchen table because I really needed to talk to him."

Roland, a Conflict Avoider, said, "I hate conflict, and I certainly didn't want to deal with Eddie's tattoo. Besides, it was done already. I'd rather work on my boat than have a 'discussion' any day. I just tuned Peggy out."

Peggy said, "It didn't take a rocket scientist to figure out Roland was avoiding me. I waited until he went down to his boat, and then I followed him there. Boy, was he angry!" Peggy laughed.

Roland admitted, "I was *not* happy. But Peggy was right; we had to talk about the kid's tattoo. Peggy was afraid next time he would do something crazier."

Peggy said, "Eddie said somebody told him, 'It's easier to seek forgiveness than get permission.' I told him that's the stupidest expression we ever heard and that in the future he had better get permission—not because the tattoo was so bad but because there are health considerations Eddie didn't even think about. Eddie thought Roland was going to go hide, as usual, but when Roland backed me up, Eddie admitted getting the tattoo was a spur-of-the-moment idea, and next time he'd take time to think first."

Conflict Innovator Quiz: Questions to Ask Yourself

Use the following questions to decide whether you are, or are not, a Conflict Innovator:

1. Do you consider all the options before engaging other people in discussion?
2. Do you bring up issues that are important to you, even if doing so makes you or others uncomfortable?
3. Do you have an inquiring mind, and are you a curious observer of social interactions?
4. Do you believe that you are a creative thinker?
5. Are you skilled at securing fair outcomes for everyone?

Journaling

In answering the preceding questions, think about the controversial issues that plague you the most. Are you weighing your answers carefully when bias abounds? Write about the difficulties you have had with people who try to control you. Are you proud of the way you handled these hassles, or do you wish you had tried another way of communicating? Write about any successes you have had in settling a conflict in a kind way.

Combining Conflict Styles

Conflict Innovators are the most consistent. If you tend to use the other styles, circumstances will help determine which one you use. Technically it's possible that you could be a combination of the following:

- A Conflict Avoider at work, where you are quiet and absorbed in the tasks at hand
- A Conflict Fixer at church, where you want everyone to see that you have the best of intentions
- A Conflict Goof-Up with your big sister, who has always tried—unsuccessfully!—to run your life
- A Conflict Antagonist with your neighbor, who parks his trucks on your lawn and has a rock band playing in his home at all hours of the night

Sometimes we shift from one conflict style into another. Conflict Avoiders, Conflict Goof-Ups, and Conflict Fixers all run the risk, when they become exasperated and cranky, of becoming full-fledged Conflict Antagonists. When Conflict Innovators lose their temper, they take a breather, put their thinking cap on, and consider more appropriate ways to approach their squabbles.

Sometimes you may switch styles over the course of a relationship or a lifetime. You may have grown up being a Conflict Avoider but recently found your voice. You may have been a quiet Conflict Avoider early in your marriage, but now you have turned into a wrathful Conflict Antagonist. Or, preferably, you may have started out a Conflict Antagonist but become an older, wiser Conflict Innovator.

Each conflict style embodies unique dimensions that determine how you will interact with the people in your world. Generally, the positive habits of each conflict style have the benefit of diminishing conflict, whereas the negative habits of each conflict style are counterproductive. As you reflect on what effect your behavior has on your loved ones and how their conduct affects you, conflicted relationships may take on a whole new meaning. In so many practical ways, knowing, understanding, and owning your conflict style(s) enables you to see yourself as others see you.

Questions for Reflection

- Now that you have read about all the conflict styles, is there any one style that best describes you? Do you alternate between different styles?
- How has your primary conflict style worked in your behalf?
- Think about your early life experiences and the conflict styles you were exposed to as a child. Do you see any connections between your childhood recollections and your current way(s) of dealing with conflict?
- What conflicted issues are most difficult for you to handle?
- What conflict style and behavior trouble you the most?
- What kind of noticeable damage occurs when you confront others?
- If you are not satisfied with your conflict style(s), are you interested in changing your primary conflict style? If so, what would that change look like?

Journaling

Write down five significant people in your life, and then note the conflict style you use with each one. If you use different conflict styles for different individuals, ask yourself why. Are you satisfied with how you have handled your contentious issues with these five people? Are there any useful techniques you could take from one situation and apply to another?

Now think about several different arguments you've had, and consider which one was your greatest success in the long run. By now you know that a "win" isn't necessarily a "success." If you have settled a conflict in a compassionate, unbiased way, write down what happened and why you think you were successful on that occasion.

Write down any significant issues that are plaguing you today. Think about how a Conflict Innovator would approach these conflicts. Write down some constructive notes.

Finally, take five minutes to write about the people you most admire and describe how they have been an inspiration to you. Then write about the important people in your life who have hurt you.

Now be proud of yourself for doing your homework. Your diligence will hold you in good stead as you learn more about resolving your disagreements.

5

How the Different Conflict Styles Interact

W hat happens when you and your husband/wife/partner/ lover/significant other have different conflict styles? Following are some stories that illustrate the conflict styles in action. Keep in mind that identifying the patterns in your relationships is the first step in solving your problems with conflict.

Scenario #1: Conflict Avoider + Conflict Avoider

When two Conflict Avoiders are together, *everything* gets swept under the rug! Sometimes Conflict Avoiders have to be persuaded that it is worth pulling their head out of the sand. It's worth noting that in the following story, it took five weeks of therapy for this Conflict Avoiding couple to address each other directly!

Office Visit: Shirley and Jacob

Shirley and Jacob had been married twenty-six years, and their first grandchild was on the way. Shirley told me, "It bothers me that Jacob doesn't talk to me and he seems so distant. I call him a loner because he spends hours on crossword puzzles, or he's in the basement working on his wood carvings. We don't have many friends because I work full-time and I keep busy cooking, sewing, and gardening. When I reach out to Jacob, the silence is deafening. I want to shake him, but he's mostly in his own world. I'm lonely. I want to share how I feel, but he's not available, so I cry a lot. I guess I'm depressed."

Shirley wept and continued with her story. "My mother was widowed shortly after her seventh child was born. Our family was poor, and there never was enough money. My mother was a seamstress; she worked hard and ran a tight ship. She favored my three older sisters and sided with them so I could never get close to any of them. I always resented my mother for that. I was the middle child, just old enough to take care of my three younger brothers, but I got lost in the shuffle. As a kid, I felt neglected because I never got the attention I desperately wanted and needed."

During her therapy sessions, Shirley cried incessantly. At first she apologized for her tears. I told Shirley not to feel guilty for crying and reassured her that she would stay healthier when she cried and released her pent-up emotions.

Shirley said, "When I talk to you, Lee, I cry, but when I'm at home, I don't cry anymore because Jacob gets too upset with me. He once told me, 'Shirley, you're a grown woman, now stop acting like a crybaby!' And after that I stopped crying when he was around."

I said, "No wonder you are lonely. You are suppressing your emotions because Jacob doesn't know how to cope with your tears."

Shirley said, "I know Jacob so well, but how do I approach him without weeping when I want him to talk to me?"

I said, "Shirley, let's make this as easy as possible. I suggest you ask Jacob if he would be willing to come to your next therapy session. Tell him that he doesn't have to say a word; all he has to do is listen and observe."

Shirley said, "It sounds risky, but I'll ask him and I won't pester him."

A week later the couple came to my office. I shook hands with Jacob and he said, "Hello, I'm pleased to meet you." We sat down and I turned my attention to Shirley, who talked and wept. I had hoped that Jacob would relent and say something, but he was mute. At the close of the meeting, I asked if he would return five more times with the understanding that he was not obliged to speak unless he had something he wanted to say. He agreed.

At the close of the fourth session, I was glad that Jacob finally spoke. He said, "So this is what therapy is about. I've always wondered."

Halfway through the fifth meeting, Jacob shared a little of his story. "I grew up in a family where no one said much. We ate our meals in silence. I was not raised with conversation just for the sake of talking. So I don't have much to say."

Shirley turned to Jacob and said, "I'm glad you told Lee something about your background." This comment encouraged Jacob to smile.

I said, "I have a suggestion that I think might help you. Take turns reading a few newspaper articles to each other two or three times a week."

Shirley immediately said, "Yes, that's OK with me."

Jacob told me, "I guess we can do this, but it never would have occurred to me. How is reading the newspaper going to help us?"

Before I could answer his question, Shirley enthusiastically said, "Well, we would share ideas and have interesting things to discuss!"

Jacob said, "Well, all right, we can do this."

Shirley dried her eyes, and the couple left my office holding hands like teenagers.

At the sixth session Jacob said, "We are making a habit of talking about current events, and we do this almost every day."

Shirley said, "Jacob and I are getting along better, too. We are talking more, and next week Jacob is interested in seeing a miniature train exhibit, so I'm going with him."

Jacob turned to me and said, "By the way, I have a question to ask you. I always thought I was supposed to fix Shirley's tears. Am I right about that?"

I said reassuringly, "Let's put it this way, Jacob. You are not responsible for fixing Shirley's tears. That's her job to do."

Jacob said, "I didn't know that. What a relief!"

Shirley listened intently and smiled as she said, "Now I don't feel so guilty when I cry, and that's a real comfort in so many ways."

Scenario #2: Conflict Fixer + Conflict Fixer

Conflict Fixers can be highly opinionated about what they believe is best for a relationship. Ironically, they run the risk of destroying the relationship with all their beneficial advice.

Office Visit: Judy and Matt

Judy and Matt had been married for five years. Both were previously divorced, so they knew more than they wanted to know about failed relationships. When the couple disagreed, they were at each other's throats because they personalized each other's words and inevitably felt rejected. They were highly opinionated Conflict Fixers, oppositional partners struggling to determine who was right and who was wrong.

Matt said, "Judy is so bossy and demanding of me. I think she should love me the way I am."

Judy said, "Matt gets so arrogant and condescending. He doesn't want to believe what I say is the truth. He doesn't trust me. He's adversarial, and so is his dad."

Matt said, "In order for me to understand Judy, she expects me to think like she thinks. So it turns out she's right and I'm wrong."

Judy said, "I'm nervous about sharing my feelings with Matt. He should give me more respect."

Matt said, "I've found out that if I express my opinions, I'm guilty 'til proven innocent."

Judy said, "When I open up to Matt, he can't deal with it. He reacts before he hears all I have to say. That makes me anxious, and that's when I cut him off."

Matt said, "I want Judy to accept me. My father didn't accept me for who I am. He was always right, and when he didn't get his way, he would fly off the handle and then my mom would start to cry. I got a lot of mixed messages from my parents."

In the course of my coaching this couple, Matt and Judy discovered that each of them was willing to look at their problems only from his or her personal point of view. The couple learned that each person was entitled to have differing opinions about their relationship. In fact, both partners might be justifiably right at the same time. If neither party accepted this truth, then both partners would clash.

Fortified with this welcome insight, Judy and Matt conceded that their partnership was far more important than arguing, and staying together was more important than who was right or wrong. They decided to invest their combined energies in building a trusting relationship one step at a time rather than tearing it to smithereens.

Scenario #3: Conflict Goof-Up + Conflict Goof-Up

One Conflict Goof-Up is enough to create chaos. Two of them can have a hard time determining what is even real!

Office Visit: Roger and Audrey

When Audrey and Roger came to see me, Audrey said, "When I don't see eye to eye with Roger, we bicker about the littlest things. He forgot to pick up my dress at the cleaners, and I was really put out. I wanted to yell at him, but I got so nervous the words wouldn't come out of my mouth. I never seem to get it right with Roger."

Roger said, "I don't get it. Why is Audrey so afraid of me? We both work hard and have good jobs, the kids are growing up, and soon we are going to be empty nesters. I don't know why she is so insecure. I'm not abusing her. But whenever I am firm with Audrey, she makes a big deal out of it. She says, 'You're shouting at me!' Give me a break."

Audrey said to Roger, "Whenever I try to communicate, you put me down. No wonder I cry myself to sleep. I'm so embarrassed that our relationship is falling apart. What kind of a life is this?"

Roger snapped, "Audrey, you are exaggerating. Here I am trying to talk to you, and instead you are making everything way too complex. It seems like whatever I have to say, it's not good enough!"

The couple shared with me that they felt guilty and ashamed of their conduct. I pointed out that they were harming their relationship by pointing fingers at each other instead of taking responsibility for their own behavior. I told them I would be willing to work with them if they were willing to work with each other. I had a feeling they would say yes because they had already taken the important first step of coming to my office together.

> This human aspect of negotiation can be either helpful or disastrous. . . . A working relationship where trust, understanding, respect and friendship are built over time can make each new negotiation smoother and more efficient. . . . On the other hand, people get angry, depressed, fearful, hostile,

frustrated and offended. They have egos that are threatened. They see the work from their vantage point. Routinely, they fail to interpret what you say in the way you intend and do not mean what you understand them to say. Misunderstandings can reinforce prejudice and lead to reactions that produce counterreactions in a vicious circle; rational exploration of possible solutions becomes impossible and a negotiation fails. The purpose of the game becomes scoring points, confirming negative impressions, and apportioning blame at the expense of the substantive interests of both parties.[2]

Scenario #4: Conflict Antagonist + Conflict Antagonist

Conflict Antagonists have an easygoing side and a hell-to-pay side. When they are defensive and cranky, they find fault with others and will not leave it alone. Two cranky Conflict Antagonists can lead to spectacles like depositing his clothes all over the front lawn or leaving her standing in the rain at the gas station. When two Conflict Antagonists duke it out, they often become estranged.

Office Visit: Jerry and Wendy

My client Jerry said, "I'm fit to be tied with Wendy. I hate it when she badgers me. Wendy insists I go to see her mother every Sunday, which is when I plan to go hiking or fishing. I work six days a week, and I look forward to my time outdoors on Sunday. We end up having a big fight, and by the time I get to my mother-in-law's home, I'm in a bad mood. Then Wendy jumps on me and says I'm acting childish."

Wendy said, "I don't think it is unreasonable to ask Jerry to visit my mother. She's an invalid, and she looks forward to our coming. We bring special foods for her, and she really appreciates what we do. I think Jerry is awfully selfish and uncaring. We argue and argue about this conflict and never seem to get anywhere. This bothers me so much that I keep getting madder and madder. Last weekend I hid Jerry's fishing gear."

Jerry said, "I do not take kindly to people messing with my things. Instead of going fishing, I went to the gym. It's hard for me to love Wendy when I'm mad at her or she's mad at me."

Wendy said, "I keep hoping there's a way out of this dark place we are in. I hate arguing, but we do it anyway, and our relationship is in very sad shape."

I said, "Have you noticed that you keep retaliating against each other? As long as you continue to pick fights with one another, you will be miserable and you will have trouble holding your relationship together. We need to introduce some strategies to help you get some of the poison out of your relationship."

Scenario #5: Conflict Innovator + Conflict Innovator

In an ideal world, everyone would be a Conflict Innovator! There would be less stress, better understanding, and more laughter.

Office Visit: Leslie and Gary

Leslie told me that five weeks after she and Gary married, they had their first uncomfortable confrontation.

Leslie said, "One evening we were cleaning up after dinner when Gary declared in his most patronizing voice, 'Leslie, I'll have you know that part of cleaning up the kitchen is mopping the floor.' My jaw just dropped. But rather than get in a fight, I just laughed and said, 'To hell with you, Gary! If you want the kitchen floor cleaned every night after dinner, then grab a mop and do it yourself!'"

Leslie told me she wasn't quite sure how Gary would take her confrontation, but she took the risk anyway. She said, "I knew Gary was loyal to me. He backed off, and we still have fun laughing over 'the mop.'"

I told the partners, "Your story is a great example of the value of confrontation, especially when you can laugh about it and stop the conflict before it gets started!"

Scenario #6: Conflict Avoider + Conflict Fixer

In this combination, one partner is eager to correct any problems as only he or she knows how, while the other doesn't even want to admit problems exist.

Office Visit: Tyler and Elaine

My client Tyler, a Conflict Fixer, said, "We aren't getting along, and our arguments are wearing me out."

Elaine, a Conflict Avoider, replied, "I really don't know why we bicker so much. We never accomplish anything."

I said, "You can argue with someone you love and still be close to them if you laugh about it later. Some people argue a great deal of the time, but it all blows over and does no permanent damage. However, aggressive arguing will inevitably test the limits of your tolerance. How much ongoing emotional battering and bruising can you endure?"

Elaine said, "Tyler and I have a missing connection. I never talk to him one-on-one anymore because he irritates my soul. If I say it's white, Tyler says it's black, and right away we argue. It's all a stupid waste of time."

Tyler said, "I want to talk it out with Elaine, but as soon as I start sharing my ideas, she shuts down."

Elaine said, "I can't stand conflict; it's not my thing. I get so mad at Tyler and his bright ideas. Then he tries to butter me up, but I see right through him. He's not fooling me!"

Tyler said, "I'm not buttering you up! It looks like our relationship is down the sewer because Elaine says she's not happy with me."

I said, "Did you know there is a correct way to argue?"

Tyler and Elaine were taken aback.

"If you follow my seven steps, you will be able to disagree without doing lasting damage to your relationship. Elaine, you will learn that conflict doesn't have to be bad. And Tyler, you will learn that everyone has a valid point of view." On hearing this, the partners laughed with relief.

Tyler said, "My friends think I'm really congenial. Come to think of it, I don't usually give them as much advice as I give Elaine."

Elaine said, "Overall, I can see we have to learn how to relate to each other when we clash. It's not like we were ever taught how to argue correctly."

Scenario #7: Conflict Avoider + Conflict Goof-Up

This is another tricky combination, because the Conflict Goof-Up probably makes life difficult for the Conflict Avoider, who is likely to seethe in silence.

Office Visit: Barbara and James

Barbara, a Conflict Avoider, told me, "I can't rely on James for anything. He just screws up everything, and then he has a boatload of excuses for not taking out the trash, for not calling me when he's coming home late, for forgetting to pick up the prescriptions at the pharmacy, and so on and so on. Yesterday he promised to pick up the dry cleaning, and I was looking forward to wearing my favorite outfit to the gallery opening, but of course he forgot. There's no point talking to him about all this stuff because he really thinks it's all my fault. Conflict with James is my worst nightmare."

James, a Conflict Goof-Up, said, "You didn't remind me about the dry cleaning. Besides, you looked fine in that black dress."

Barbara said, "I don't know what's the matter with James, but I'm not satisfied with him, and he's mad at me. I feel as if we are stuck, and I don't know where to go from here to make our relationship OK."

James said, "I think our relationship is pretty good, except that you're so cranky all the time." Barbara looked at James as if her head was going to explode.

I said, "James, has anyone besides Barbara ever commented about your absentmindedness? Or maybe said something about your time management?"

James said, "Well, actually, I lost a client because they said I never turned my work in on time. But it wasn't my fault; they kept changing their deadlines. And besides, I know they had a lot of air in their schedules so they didn't have to be so strict."

I said, "Barbara and James, I am assuming you want to work on your relationship because you are here in my office. To begin, let's spend some time clarifying the issues that Barbara perceives but won't discuss. Then we'll see how James feels about the same topics."

Scenario #8: Conflict Fixer + Conflict Goof-Up

Conflict Goof-Ups naturally make a mess of almost everything, while Conflict Fixers want to sort out anything they can. When one person likes to make messes and the other likes to clean them up, there is endless strife.

Office Visit: Lisa and Tammy

My client Lisa, a financial adviser, is a Conflict Fixer. She had recently joined a new firm as a partner. She said, "Tammy, my assistant, is driving me nuts. The firm assigned her to me when I arrived, and she has been taking it easy ever since. She leaves the office early and doesn't tell me why. She calls in to say she'll be late, and sometimes she doesn't show up at all. I can't work like this!"

Lisa's faced was flushed when I asked her if she had confronted Tammy. Lisa looked like she was about to cry when she said, "Yes, I did confront her, and I told her all the things she needed to do correctly. I ran through my expectations for her professional behavior. She said her former boss came and went as he pleased and he let Tammy do the same. She said I never explained to her what I wanted, so it wasn't her fault I was upset. Meanwhile I'm having a fit because Tammy isn't getting some vital reports out on time. She takes forever to do even simple tasks, and I keep having to ask her to retype letters and reports because she never gets anything right the first time. Her workload is piling up. I'm upset about confronting Tammy a second time because I don't know how to approach her any differently."

I said, "Lisa, I know you are frustrated with Tammy. She sounds like a Conflict Goof-Up to me, which means you have your work cut out for you. It is hard to hold Conflict Goof-Ups accountable for their actions, and they tend to get very defensive, very quickly. I recommend you say something encouraging, like, 'Tammy, you are a valuable employee with a long track record of success.' Then set up a meeting with her to talk about all the sticky issues. This will confirm your authority and hopefully will short-circuit Tammy's inclination to throw everything back on you. In the meantime, start a file about Tammy's shortcomings. You may need it."

Lisa's face lit up, and she said, "I can do that!"

Scenario #9: Conflict Avoider + Conflict Antagonist

The Conflict Avoider just wants to keep the peace, while the Conflict Antagonist just wants to have a fight. Can two people at such cross-purposes coexist? In his book *Healing from Family Rifts*, clinical social worker Mark Sichel explains, "Declaring one's autonomy is a surefire way to ignite the furies of the family member who greedily desires to have the psychological upper hand over all who claim to love him or her."[1]

Office Visit: Bette and John

My clients Bette, a Conflict Avoider, and John, a Conflict Antagonist, were often at odds with each other.

Bette said, "When John asked me why I was so annoyed, I honestly told him in no uncertain terms, 'You are out of line and you're upsetting me.' Then without giving me a chance to explain more, John jumped all over me, accusing me of being selfish and a troublemaker. I'm overpowered and I can't stand up to this jerk. Sometimes I don't talk to John for a week or more. I know there's something radically amiss, but I don't know what to do."

It hadn't occurred to Bette that when she tried to confront John and he upbraided her, she was pitted against a Conflict Antagonist. Although John said he loved Bette, he was so quick to find fault with her that she wondered if this could possibly be true. Being a Conflict Avoider, Bette said nothing for years, but in the meantime her anger smoldered under the surface. If this relationship was going to survive, I knew we would have to find strategies for Bette to use other than the silent treatment, and we would need to get John to stop and think before saying any more damaging remarks.

Scenario #10: Conflict Fixer + Conflict Antagonist

Conflict Fixers have an exaggerated view of their own talent for correcting what's wrong with their relationships. Conflict Antagonists usually have an exaggerated and exasperated view of what's wrong.

Office Visit: Arthur

Arthur, an industrial manager of a large construction company, was doing some technical work for me, and when he was finished, we chatted briefly. I was at my desk and offhandedly mentioned the title of this book. Arthur confessed, "I honestly hate conflict!" As he started to give me his impressions of conflict, I was so intrigued that I interrupted him and asked if I could write down his story word for word, and he agreed.

"I deal with a lot of customers," Arthur began, "and I know everybody has issues, but some people are just looking for an argument. They thrive on 'I'm right, you're wrong' conflicts. All they would have to do is talk to me and ask me questions, and if I'm wrong, I'll admit it. It seems to me in this day and age that the customer is not always right. I can't deal with the right/wrong stuff! It bothers me, because if the people would be honest and nice about it, we could resolve their issues very easily. But they are always looking for a fight!"

I asked Arthur how he was affected by his customers who are so hostile. He said, "For me, when they display their animosity, the stress is beyond belief. It's such an energy drainer. It makes me tense, I can't think straight, and it's just not necessary! Sometimes my customers drive me to distraction."

I told Arthur that these people fit the Conflict Antagonist style, and I wanted to know more about how he relates to them.

Arthur said, "Half the time I find out they don't mean to be as rude as they sound because they usually have other things in their life troubling them. And they don't mean to take it out on other people, but they just do. I've noticed some people have too many irons in the fire that they have to deal with and that puts them in a bad mood."

My next question was, "So how do you handle these situations?"

Arthur replied, "I don't let other people's vindictive attitude bother me. I won't let it eat at me because I know they don't mean it. I don't hold it against them either. I was raised human like everyone else, and fortunately, I learned from my dad about how people are. And a lot of times, you aren't going to be able to change these people and that's how it is!

"The way I see it, most of the people who are argumentative have inherited their money. They treat people differently. They don't seem to care about others—it's just what they want that counts. I know they are venting anger at me because I'm the one who is available at the time. I don't personalize it when they are not nice.

"But people who get their money the old-fashioned way—they work for it—these people are easier to deal with. They are honest and disciplined, and they usually treat other people respectfully, like you want to be treated yourself."

I mentioned the five conflict styles, and without skipping a beat Arthur said, "Sure, I'm a Conflict Fixer. If my customers are having a bad day, I ask them what's wrong and I try to fix it. My cup is always half full because things could always be worse. I'm easy to talk to, and I listen to my customers' stories. I care about them. I have so many customers, and I remember their problems and the next time I see them, I ask if our products are working for them. They are surprised that I remember their name, and they appreciate that."

As our conversation closed, I said, "Arthur, you have an astute way of listening with intention. You are curious about people, and you have so much compassion for mankind. I would say you are a prospective Conflict Innovator because you know the rules for getting along with people so well. Bless you for sharing your story, because others can learn from your experience."

Scenario #11: Conflict Goof-Up + Conflict Antagonist

Conflict Goof-Ups get everything mixed up but try to wriggle out of taking responsibility for the confusion they cause. Conflict Antagonists are only too happy to assign blame, finding fault even where none exists. Unfortunately for the Conflict Antagonist, arguing with a Conflict Goof-Up is like nailing Jell-O to the wall.

Office Visit: Jack and Maria

Jack is a minister with a devoted parish. He is an active member of the local community. Jack radiates warmth and caring, delivers thoughtful and inspiring sermons on Sundays, and is always available for families or individuals in crisis. Jack has something of an absentminded professor reputation because he tends to forget appointments and directions. Jack's parishioners have no idea how forgetful he really is.

Jack's wife, Maria, married Jack for love, not stopping for a moment to wonder what life with Jack was going to be like twenty or thirty years down the road. Maria loves Jack, but she does not love being a minister's wife, particularly when the minister in question never remembers to buy gas, pick up the kids at school, or mail important packages.

When Jack and Maria first came to my office, I thought they were a delightful couple. Jack saw a special picture on my wall and immediately went into a long, scholarly tangent that I found fascinating, until Maria's pained expression brought me back to reality. Maria snapped, "I can't believe you are wasting our time with another one of your stupid diatribes."

Jack looked mildly surprised and answered, "I was just talking about Lee's picture. What's wrong with that?"

Maria hissed, "You know that's not why we are here. We're here because you are such a screwup."

I interrupted and suggested we start over.

Maria, a Conflict Antagonist, did not hesitate to confront Jack on a daily basis about his shortcomings—and there were many. I could see that Maria was not able to share any of the parenting or household chores with Jack because he would always end up three blocks away, comforting a parishioner instead. Jack, a Conflict Goof-Up, professed to be confused by Maria's anger. He was just doing his job; Maria had known what she was getting into when they married. Her life was much like the lives of other ministers' wives. Why was she so whiny?

I suggested to Jack and Maria that, inside the safe environment of my office, we would begin to explore whether or not Maria's critical remarks were in fact justified. Both partners needed to take more responsibility for their roles in the situation. A professional reality check might be all they needed in order to get back on track.

Scenario #12: Conflict Avoider + Conflict Innovator

We know that Conflict Innovators take a mature, caring approach to disputes. But what happens when a Conflict Innovator is paired up with a Conflict Avoider, who just wants to be left alone and keep the peace?

Office Visit: Marie and David

Marie said, "David, it isn't fair that your mother gives you money, and she gives your kids tons of gifts, but she won't spend a nickel on *my* kids because they are her stepgrandchildren."

David, a Conflict Avoider, said, "Let's be fair. I can't tell my mother what to do, and if I did, she would have a fit. You know that I'm trying to hold our family together the best way I can."

Marie declared, "Dana assumes she can run our family because she's not thinking about *our* marriage, *our* relationship, *our* children. She just pretends I don't exist. She's the one who is tearing us apart." I thought Marie showed Conflict Innovator fairness when she purposely did not blame David for the problem with his mother.

David protested, "Marie, since you think my mother isn't fair with her gifts, I think *you* should tell her, because I'm not touching this conflict with a ten-foot pole!"

I told David and Marie that I had an idea that had the potential to work out well for everyone. Then I asked David, "Would you be willing to approach Dana, with Marie and you being teammates together?"

Before I could say another word, David interrupted, "I don't know what you are up to, Lee, but I'm not getting sucked into something like this!"

I persevered and said, "I'll explain how this strategy works best." I turned to Marie and said, "I suggest that you and David stand together as teammates and you say, 'Dana, David and I would appreciate it if you would give *our seven children* a small gift costing no more than five dollars for special holidays like Christmas, Easter, and other special events. Then each grandchild would be happy and none of our children will be left out.'"

Marie said, "I like this plan. It is not confrontational. We're not saying how mean she is. And it would be super if my kids could feel included instead of ignored."

David hesitated before saying, "I hate conflict so much that the very thought of the two of us confronting my mother gives me a headache."

I said, "David, you know you are a Conflict Avoider, so this strategy probably seems radical to you. However, think about the damage you are doing to your stepkids because Marie and you have tolerated Dana's unfairness for the last five years. You know Marie's children have been treated like they don't exist. I'm wondering if you have ever been treated unfairly?"

David said, "Of course I have. I got a rotten break when I didn't make my high school basketball team. All right, I see your point! If Marie does the talking with my mom and I'm standing beside her, then we won't be bickering about this conflict anymore."

The partners followed through with this strategy and were relieved when Dana grudgingly agreed to their request. In turn, Marie's children gradually began to feel as if they belonged to their stepdad's side of the family, and the parents were relieved that this conflict was finally resolved.

Scenario #13: Conflict Fixer + Conflict Innovator

The big difference between a Conflict Fixer and a Conflict Innovator is that a Conflict Fixer has an exaggerated idea of his or her own talents at handling conflict. The Conflict Fixer may create more problems than he or she solves.

Office Visit: Douglas and Esther

Douglas, a Conflict Innovator, didn't know how to respond to his inquisitive wife, Esther, a Conflict Fixer, who had a lot of questions about his psychotherapy sessions. Esther was curious and wanted to talk to him about what he was telling his counselor. She thought maybe she could help, and she offered Douglas a few ideas of her own. Esther wasn't sure she liked Douglas's therapist, and in any case she felt she knew Douglas better than the therapist did. Who better to help him with his problems?

Douglas didn't want to hurt Esther's feelings, but neither did he want to tell her more than necessary. So he said, "Esther, I'm not skilled enough to know how to respond to you right now. I am learning a lot, but let's put this conversation on hold until I am better prepared to answer your questions."

This maintained Douglas's privacy and effectively shut down Esther's intrusion without making her feel insulted.

Scenario #14: Conflict Goof-Up + Conflict Innovator

Conflict Goof-Ups try the nerves of all their closest friends and family members. Handling the infinite screwups and accusations is a challenge even for the wise Conflict Innovator.

Office Visit: Sheldon and Abbie

Sheldon, a Conflict Goof-Up, told me, "I have felt pressure from my dad all my life. I was never good enough for him. If I got a B in math, he would say it should have been an A. When I took second place in the track meet, he said I screwed up and should have been first. My dad wasn't that way with my sister, but for whatever reason he had it in for me. It sure hasn't done much for my self-esteem.

"I do sculptures, I write a lot of fiction, but I never complete any of the projects I start because I'm afraid of failing. I don't accomplish any of my goals. I've been depressed off and on—that's why I have isolated myself. I'm ashamed of myself, and I guess that's why I don't respect myself.

"I know I'm babbling a lot, but if I have all these fears, how can I have a good relationship with my partner, Abbie? She keeps obsessing about her career, and she's often distracted and not thinking about me."

Abbie said, "How can I have a good relationship with my fiancé when he is so absorbed with all his failures? Sheldon is sweet, but he seems to be preoccupied with all his projects that never seem to quite work out. I try to help him with his troubles, but he gets irritated and then we go to bed angry, and that's the pits."

Abbie, a Conflict Innovator, continued, "I'm worried that Sheldon needs more time and attention than I can reasonably give him. I thought I was getting a mature guy, not a one-man rescue mission. I'm going to do what I can to support and praise Sheldon, and maybe that will bolster his self-esteem. I'll try it for the next three months. If he is still needy and depressed after that, we'll have to reassess the direction of our relationship."

Scenario #15: Conflict Antagonist + Conflict Innovator

Conflict Innovators try to take a reasonable and equitable approach to any dispute, while Conflict Antagonists will lash out just for the sake of drawing blood. Here is a story about a Conflict Innovator who found a way to tame the savage beast.

Office Visit: Adam and Dawson

My client, Adam, had a fascinating story to tell me about his father-in-law, Dawson. Adam said, "You know I'm a good-natured guy. When Louise and I married, I looked forward to having a great relationship with my father-in-law, Dawson. We would visit several times a year, and what a disappointment he turned out to be. It really bothered me for a long time, because Dawson is such a grumpy control freak. His wife passed away ten years ago, and he lives alone on a big lake. I know he has plenty of money because he keeps himself busy with his cabin cruiser, but he hasn't much to say to me.

"Dawson is fussy and in his own world. He won't let me help him; he's too persnickety. It makes me mad because we have such different personalities and it's hard for us to relate. I'm easygoing, and he's testy and difficult. We are so incompatible I dread our visits with him."

I told Adam, "Perhaps you can find some common interest that you might have with Dawson. Then you could share your experiences and your communication will improve." Adam scratched his head and drew a blank. Then I said, "Perhaps you will think of something later—just wait."

It was six weeks later when I spoke with Adam, and he had a big grin on his face as he said, "I did what you said, and one day out of the blue it occurred to me that Dawson and I could play Scrabble. On my next visit, Dawson wasn't enthusiastic about Scrabble, but we played for an hour and it was better than not conversing with him when he's in a sour mood.

"The next time our family visited Dawson, I suggested we take a trip to the marina to see the exotic fish. We did that and he didn't talk much, but it was pleasant enough.

"A month later I happened to be traveling nearby on business, so I called Dawson and asked him if he would like to go hiking with me the next day. I was testing him. I knew he wasn't active except for keeping his boat in tiptop shape. Much to my surprise, Dawson took me up on the offer. The next day, there he was, all decked out with spiffy walking shoes and a hand-carved walking cane. He loosened up some, and he even laughed at my jokes. Since then, I've talked to Dawson by phone, we've shared a few e-mails now and then, and we are more compatible and not so distant anymore."

I said, "Adam, what a great story! You treated Dawson respect-fully, you paid attention to him, and you made friends with him. Best of all, you made peace with yourself, and that is quite an achievement!"

Questions for Reflection

- How do you handle another person's threats?
- Do you put pressure on others to do your bidding?
- Do you make threats and expect that you will follow through, or are they just hot air?
- Do you fight fairly or fight to win?
- Do you get into squabbles and then find you haven't a clue how to unravel them?
- When you are feeling down in the dumps because you are hurt and struggling, what helps you regain your composure?

Journaling

As you answer the preceding questions, write about how upset you get when your conflicted relationships are not working out. Take note of your primary and secondary conflict styles, and write about what makes you stuck so you can't seem to get past being resentful with a loved one or coworker. Then write about the people in your life who have been cruel or friendly to you and how you feel toward them. Finally, turn your attention to what you are grateful for, and write about the people in your life who have been your strongest supporters. Note if your moods go up and down as you write about the conflicted issues that matter so much to you.

I applaud you for your diligence in keeping up with your journal!

6

The Seven Essential Steps to Managing Conflict Constructively

You picked up this book because you hate conflict, but in your heart of hearts you know you have to learn how to deal with it. By now you have read the earlier chapters about the obvious and not-so-obvious causes of conflict in your life, and you have identified your personal conflict style(s)—your way of coping when you can't escape an argument or a confrontation.

In this chapter, you will learn seven steps that will serve you well in any dispute. These steps will help you do the following:

- Defuse minor conflicts
- De-escalate conflicted situations that have gotten supercharged
- Approach disagreements in an affirmative, optimistic way
- Shape your conversations in a manner that maximizes mutual understanding
- Use conflict as a positive force for change in your life

I encourage you to look at conflicts as opportunities. Using the following seven steps—not necessarily in order—you will be able to move your life in a positive direction *and* free up time and energy so you can live your life to the fullest!

1. Speak politely; common courtesies count.
2. Swallow your pride, and admit your mistakes.
3. Seek to understand; you have nothing to defend.
4. Show compassion, and keep the welfare of others in mind.
5. Be honest, and earn the trust others place in you.
6. Never wave a red flag at a raging bully.
7. Use encouragement and laughter to keep conflict at bay.

You can handle all of these seven steps, right?

If they seem somewhat obvious, let me ask you this: how often have you been engaged in a disagreement where the other side behaved with dignity and compassion? Most people do not know how to discuss their differences constructively. You're going to show them how.

Step 1: Speak Politely; Common Courtesies Count

Trusted relationships are destroyed when you complacently believe, "I can say whatever I want to say and do whatever I want to do and get away with it." Well, that might be true if you are a recluse, but you are out in left field if you expect to have meaningful, caring relationships when you deliberately defend yourself by verbally attacking your loved ones. Some people seem to be blind to understanding that a devil-may-care attitude—and the corresponding actions—is exactly why people end up in a toxic wasteland of failed relations. An aggressive defense is not a viable way to address your conflicted concerns. On the other hand, when you are forthright and sincerely tell others what is on your mind, they generally listen to you as long as you are not sassy or rude to them.

If you are afraid of being intimidated, this is reflected in your attitude. Whether it is negative, hopeful, guarded, or engaging, your attitude usually foretells the outcome of your choices. When your attitude is pessimistic, your malicious scowl expresses your disapproval and contempt for loved ones or peers. When you maintain a positive attitude, your welcoming smile, engaging handshake, and enjoyable laughter are contagious.

This first step is paramount when you are stymied by your conflicted situations. As you mind your manners and speak politely to others in a well-modulated voice, it's relatively easy to get along. When you find yourself in a conflicted situation, your behavior makes it clear that you understand the meaning of decorum by being tactful, discreet, and prudent.

Simple good manners go a long way in terms of resolving your differences effectively. Common courtesies count because discussing your disputes in a reasonable manner requires a cordial approach. Speaking politely makes it possible for you to confront your loved ones and coworkers without humiliating them or doing them any harm. Your unassuming, down-to-earth approach to negotiating your differences must be respectful to others at all times.

Kerry Patterson's book *Crucial Conversations* discusses the nature of respect and the challenge of showing respect for people you don't respect:

> When we recognize that we all have weaknesses, it's easier to find a way to respect others. When we do this, we feel a kinship, a sense of mutuality between ourselves and even the thorniest of people.[1]

When appropriate etiquette and respect are lacking, verbal assaults are often repeated daily. Unfortunately, the language of the streets is reinforced by the media that chips away at genteel communication. As kids mimic their friends' raunchy language and behavior, they speak the rude language of whatever is the fad of the day. And all too soon, young adults are just as cynical and calculating as their parents, pals, and others who take a "so what" irreverent attitude. Instead of acts of kindness and respect, many people are determined to utilize their power through cunning manipulation that they justify by their egotistical and arrogant posture. Conflict escalates whenever people take a ruthless position that stretches the limits of tolerance to include harsh, uncompromising behavior. Bad manners complicate matters as Conflict Antagonists get angry and start fights while Conflict Avoiders back off and keep their distance.

Wisdom suggests that you bravely take the first step as a challenge to clean up your act by using diplomacy and good judgment when tackling your conflicts. There is no way to settle your disagreements unless you maintain your dignity. Your courteous approach and respectful language sets the stage for taking a firm, constructive stance in negotiating your disputes. In all your daily social interactions, be smart enough to know that any hostile vulgarities will take you down the low road and destroy any hope of having healthy relations with the most important people in your life.

I can't say it often enough: be polite to everyone, but in particular, be sensitive to how you treat the people you profess to love. The more you demonstrate your integrity, the more you stop rehashing old battles, the more time and energy you will have not only to address your current conflicts but also to pursue activities you enjoy.

Questions for Reflection

- What did your parents teach you about proper manners in your home?
- Is proper decorum used in your workplace?
- What are your conversations like when you are unclear what you want?
- Are you respectful when you speak to angry people?
- Are you aware of being cynical and sarcastic when you are annoyed with others?

Take two minutes to also reflect on the following three provocative questions:

1. When you verbally attack your loved ones, what do you expect to get in return?
2. When you offend others, do you expect them to do you favors?
3. When you don't take responsibility for your actions, what are the consequences of your conduct?

Journaling

As you answer the preceding questions, write about your experiences with the special people in your life and describe how etiquette, or the lack of it, factor into your conversations. Pay close attention to your interactions with others when they are rude, and then write about how you respond, be it politely or crudely. It takes guts to do this work, but keep in mind that you are working on improving your relationships, not tossing them to the winds.

Step 2: Swallow Your Pride, and Admit Your Mistakes

The logical purpose of the second step is to acknowledge your faults, knowing full well that you are no different from anyone else.

You heap more conflict on yourself when you insist on being self-righteously "right" and persist in declaring the other person is "wrong, wrong, wrong!" That is the quickest way I know to immediately alienate the people in your life who you aim to impress. It's not a big deal to say something like the following:

- "I'm really sorry that I made a mistake, and I will rectify it by doing the best I can to . . ."
- "I regret that I wasn't thinking about what I said or how I came across to you."
- "I apologize for being flippant and hurting your feelings."
- "I know I have a sharp tongue, so I need to be more careful and tone it down whenever we disagree."

- "I realize my hostile demeanor is upsetting to others, so I promise to curb my temper."

Anytime you try to prove that you are right and try to convince others that they are wrong, you are barking up the wrong tree. To get the conversation or relationship back on track, you will need to acknowledge your arrogance, express your regret, and indicate how you plan to make amends.

Right or Wrong?

The second step presents a daunting question: would you rather be right or be happy? It's a lonesome road when you don't recognize that, like all humanity, you never achieve an optimum state of perfection in every aspect of your life because we all make mistakes. In the real world of conflicted issues, do not make the erroneous assumption that you know it all. Controlling folks indulge in wishing, thinking, and wanting to know it all, but deep down in their belly, they are just plain scared of being wickedly wrong.

The second step is essential if you hope to achieve closure and put your conflicts to rest. It is imperative that you dig a little deeper and understand that when you are unable to admit your mistakes in judgment and conduct, you are taking incredible risks with your closest relations. Anytime you refuse to say, "I'm sorry, I was wrong, and I won't do that again," you are making one of the biggest mistakes of your life. By acknowledging your errors, you gain the admiration and respect of others, and that makes it possible to resolve your conflicts in a reasonable manner.

In *Healing the Heart of Conflict*, Marc Gopin gives us some answers to the right-or-wrong dilemma:

> Conflict is confusing precisely because in most situations there is *not* a perfectly clear way to assign blame. It is extremely difficult for even the most seasoned and moral

judges to figure out who is more right in most situations—it depends on your point of view. Also, more often than not we are so distracted in conflict by the hurt of someone's assault on us that we cannot even begin to examine our own role in the conflict. We are too busy defending ourselves or preparing our own attack.[2]

Judge and Jury

We make all kinds of judgments about ourselves and others based on our life experiences. When we judge others and they judge us, everybody feels entitled to their own interpretation of what is right, correct, or fair. We hurt others either by accident, because we don't realize what we are saying, or deliberately, because we are feeling mean-spirited and don't care.

When we believe we are right, we feel innocent, like we are the injured party. When we assume innocence at all costs, we are apt to take a holier-than-thou attitude and refuse to fess up to our errors in judgment and conduct. Sometimes we put on this facade to cover up our deep-seated insecurities. For example, Conflict Goof-Ups insist on being right when they secretly know they are wrong.

We should not be so certain of our impartiality, because we are getting only fragments of the truth about our conflicts. We are virtually walking down a blind alley, because our understanding is so limited. I often remind my clients that we can't see in back of us the way dolphins can. A dolphin's-eye view has a 180-degree arc that is coordinated to see above, below, and on both sides. Humans, both literally and figuratively, have only a partial view of the broad picture.

When you take on the role of judge and jury:

- You assume your perspective is right and another's point of view is wrong.
- You filter out contradicitons to your version of reality.

- You are hypercritical of others.
- You carry a chip on your shoulder and hold grudges.
- You distort what you said or did.
- You disregard the consequences of your controversies.
- You forgo the likelihood of resolving your differences amicably.

Saving Face

Most of us would like to preserve some semblance of self-esteem and dignity. We are interested in saving face because we want to appear admirable, virtuous, and right.

I asked my fourteen-year-old grandson, Cale, what *saving face* meant to him. He said, "Well, you don't want to look foolish in the eyes of others when you've done something bad."

I said, "I'm impressed with your astute response. In fact, many of us try to save face because we have a compulsive yearning to be thought of as blameless."

Cale nodded and said, "So we want to get a reputation for being right even if we aren't doing right."

I said, "Exactly! In fact, when we are conflicted, we are inclined to get aggressive and defensive."

Cale said, "Tell me about it. I'm not thinking I'm defensive with Mom and Dad, but I guess I am wrong about that."

The book *Getting to Yes: Negotiating Agreement Without Giving In* gives us a perspective to ponder:

> Face-saving reflects a person's need to reconcile the stand he takes in a negotiation or an agreement with his principles and with his past words and deeds. . . . Often in a negotiation people will continue to hold out not because the proposal on the table is inherently unacceptable, but simply because they want to avoid the feeling or the appearance of backing down to the other side.[3]

As you can see, figuring out who is right and who is wrong gets really messy, particularly when you thoughtlessly twist your version of reality in order to save face.

Taking Responsibility

It is only after we reflect on the consequences of our behavior that we can determine whether our actions were sensible or shameful. The upside of making mistakes is learning from each slipup we make.

When you are in the throes of conflict, it is imperative that you act with integrity by taking responsibility for your actions; foremost, be accountable by acknowledging your indiscretions. To drop your defensive stance:

- Recognize that (in some cases) you are in danger of losing your best friends.
- Admit that your opinions are just opinions that often differ from another's outlook.
- Acknowledge that you are human and are thus judgmental and biased.
- Take responsibility for the harm you did to others.
- Apologize sincerely.
- Be honest and reaffirm your credibility.
- Earnestly make amends and move on without looking backward.

When you follow these guidelines, you help others save face and spare yourself considerable grief. When there are divergent opinions, be a wise Conflict Innovator, and permit others to be right for them and you be right for you. This strategy simplifies your life and keeps your loved ones and best friends satisfied.

Questions for Reflection

- Has "being right" been a problem for you?
- Do you have trouble admitting to others that you were wrong?
- How do you relate to your close associates when you think they are being unreasonable? Do you argue with them and try to prove you are right and they are wrong?
- Are you likely to fault others when you are unhappy with them?
- Is it easy or difficult for you to say, "I'm sorry, and I won't do that again"?

Journaling

Take two minutes out of your busy schedule to consider what saving face means to you. Then write about what went "right" and what went "wrong" for you today. Inasmuch as this is a critical topic to explore, take your time to mull over the nuances of the issues that surface. Other questions might pop into your head, too. Write them down so you won't forget. Be assured that the right/wrong dilemma is a universal dilemma that gets a lot of people tied in knots. Do your best to write about your personal experiences and ideas as you dig into this weighty matter.

Giving others the right to be right until they discover otherwise is sage advice. To make that all-important apology, see Chapter 8. Mending fences could be easier than you think.

Step 3: Seek to Understand; You Have Nothing to Defend

Some people don't comprehend that being defensive is a thoughtless, reckless, irresponsible, immature type of behavior. In truth, defending oneself is so commonplace that there is a tendency to be complacent about the damage it perpetrates in every arena of a person's life. Anytime you are stubbornly defensive and adamantly uncompromising, you screw up your relationships.

If you hope to get along with the people you live with, work with, and play with, notice how your defensive behavior affects others. When you are ready to put a stop to defending yourself, you can start repairing your conflicted relationships. My clients have learned that saying to themselves, "I have nothing to defend," is a remarkably freeing experience.

When you discuss your disagreements with another and firmly say out loud, "I have nothing to defend," then immediately that person knows you are being open-minded and forthright. You remind others that there are ways to spare everyone considerable grief, distress, and needless arguing.

Don't Let Defensive Behavior Ruin Your Relationships

My friend Rose wisely said, "Thinking you are right is not the same as doing right." Clearly, you are trapped when you insist that you are right and your adversary is wrong. If you are determined to take an oppositional stance, this puts you on the defensive right away.

The dictionary defines *defensiveness* as "constantly feeling under attack and hence quick to justify one's actions . . . on the defensive . . . resisting or being ready to resist attack or danger."[4] When we are on the defensive, it means we have dug in our heels and committed ourselves to defending our position. We believe we have the right to strike, and to strike back, as needed. We have made up our minds that we are clever and right and the other person is irrational and wrong. Defensive behavior puts up walls between individuals and quickly leads to angry remarks. No one is thinking about the consequences of their inappropriate behavior, and neither person is taking responsibility for the harm done to each other.

Denial

If you have decided that you are right and the other person is wrong, what do you do when some information comes along that threatens your point of view?

You ignore it.

Denial is a defense we all use when we aren't at ease with our uncomfortable thoughts and emotions. Occasionally denial is a defense mechanism that allows people to forget heinous events so they can keep on functioning. More often, however, it is a ploy we use to avoid admitting our mistakes.

The following futile discussion represents one of the many inane ways we use denial:

She said, "You weren't nice to my mother, and I'm aggravated with you."

He said, "How can you say that? I was not nasty to your mother."

She said, "Yes, you were. You were rude to her several times."

He said, "I don't believe what I am hearing. Are you trying to drive me nuts?"

She said, "How can you *not* remember? You made an
awful scene!"

He said, "Come on, you're making that up."

Losing patience, she said, "You're just pretending you
don't know what I'm talking about."

He replied, "You're crazy, and it's time for me to go to bed!"

She muttered, "I give up! You pull this trick on me all the
time."

There are times when our memory plays tricks on us and we
truly don't remember certain conversations or events. The culprit is not always denial. For example, sometimes we are forgetful
because of stress, anxiety, or even illness. However, when people
just happen to forget information that would make them look
mistaken or even ridiculous, they may have put up an impen-
etrable mental barrier. Much like the Mad Hatter's tea party in
Alice's Adventures in Wonderland, a rational conversation is out of
the question.

There is a subtle distinction between not being ready to discuss
our controversies and refusing to talk about them at all. When we
are in denial, we add more layers of conflict that we then haphaz-
ardly shove aside.

Rationalizing

When we rationalize, we are trying to conceal our underlying
intentions. However, others are quick to catch on to this trick, so
we are only fooling ourselves.

Rationalizing is used to make whatever we want appear acceptable, even brilliant. If I see a hand-knit sweater on sale, I can easily
rationalize that (1) the sale price is unbeatable, (2) it is a unique

item I may never find again, (3) the color is extraordinary, (4) the size is perfect, (5) I've been meaning to buy a new sweater, and (6) I can afford it because one of these days my book advance is going to show up in my mailbox. By this time the clerk is wrapping the sweater in tissue paper. The truth is, I don't have the money yet, and I did not come into the store looking for a sweater at all, but these little details are not going to come between me and my new beautiful sweater.

We rationalize how we will spend our money, how we will rear our children, and how we play favorites—for example, doing more for our parents than for our in-laws. We rationalize that our boss won't be upset if we are late to a meeting, or it doesn't really matter if the report is turned in a day late. Often there are repercussions. Irritations proliferate and tempers flare.

If you fail to understand that others are going to mistrust you when you rationalize, then I recommend that you clean up your act and start being honest. Your far-fetched explanations and implausible excuses are not going to win you any friends. Courteous Conflict Innovators might say, "Let's be reasonable about who is right and who is wrong and agree to get on with our lives."

Questions for Reflection

- How often do you get defensive with others?
- What behaviors of others provoke you?
- What conduct of yours gets others mad at you?
- Are you aware when you are defensive that you are hurting yourself the most?
- What happens when you converse with another and both of you are scared and angry?

Journaling

This is really a splendid opportunity to write down your answers to the preceding questions and then take about five minutes to observe the ways you have been defensive. Next, consider whether you are ready to say to another, "I have nothing to defend." Even if this statement appears to be somewhat vague, actually you are empowered by it, because it has the greatest impact when you say these words out loud. Then write about your experiences with others who have been defensive with you or with whom you have been defensive.

Step 4: Show Compassion, and Keep the Welfare of Others in Mind

This step takes you on a journey of comprehending the emotional nuances of your conflicted relationships. A self-centered stance does not bode well for resolving interpersonal conflicts. Expecting others to have the same level of interest in satisfying your needs and desires is irrational. As you keep the welfare of others in mind, you reduce conflict by sending the message, "I'm working with you, not against you." In this way you reach out to your close associates and let them know that you are available to hold their hand, if need be, when they are immersed in worrisome conflicts.

To some extent we are all obliged to be self-absorbed, to ensure we take care of our own basic needs for body, psyche, and soul. An egocentric mind-set places us in the middle of our own little world and puts our needs ahead of those of anyone else. In the early seventies, the "me-generation" mind-set took hold with a vengeance as selfishness was lauded and carried to an extreme. This was not the decade for negotiating conflicts with empathy and understanding.

Listen carefully to how you speak. If you are focused on "me" to the exclusion of "we," then you might be a bit too narrow-minded and arrogant for your own good. Your attempts to resolve your differences might fail because you are showing too little empathy or caring concern for others.

When empathy is in short supply, people become rigid and inflexible, making it difficult to have commonsense discussions. Negotiations break down anytime you are invested in "me, me, me," to the exclusion of others. When you give little or no thought to what your adversary requests at the bargaining table, then don't be shocked when your negotiations fall apart.

When my clients display a "me first, the hell with you" attitude, I ask them to think about Core Truth #3, You Are the Center of Your World, but You Are Not the Center of the Universe (see Chapter 7). Once you acknowledge this truth, you are able to look at conflict from different perspectives. As you take a broader view of your disputes, you open your eyes and perceive not only more information about the subject at hand but also more observations about what is right and gratifying in your closest connections. Placing your loyalty to others first, not last, enables you to overlook their foibles. Daniel Goleman, eminent author of *Social Intelligence*, affirms the need for us to heed Step 4 and demonstrate our caring for others:

Empathy plays a pivotal role in care giving, which after all centers on responding to the needs of others rather than our own. Compassion, a grand term, in its everyday guise can show as availability, sensitivity, or responsiveness—all signs of good parenting or friendship. And when it comes to a prospective mate, remember, both men and women rate kindness as the number-one trait they seek.[5]

There is a famous quote from the Dalai Lama: "Be kind whenever possible. It is always possible." In terms of ultimately healing your own personal wounds, there are multiple ways to be compassionate. The Golden Rule—"Do unto others as you would have them do unto you"—will make the most sense as you recognize the value of your empathy to soothe a loved one's aching heart.

Compassionate Communication

Not everyone is a skilled communicator. Many of us are shy and reticent. Others are brusque bullies who toot their horn too loud. Some people barely speak at all, and others are compulsive talkers.

Compassionate communication is an opportunity for you to speak of your trials and tribulations, reveal your vulnerabilities, speak your inner truths, and learn more about others. Essentially, making peace with others isn't feasible if you don't have some sense of what they are experiencing. In *Healing the Heart of Conflict*, Marc Gopin explains:

> To understand both our own needs and those of someone who is actively opposing us or hating us is an agonizing moment of truth, a moment in which the world seems to be a flawed and tragic place of contradiction. . . . In conflict, once you really know your own heart, and when you come to know the heart of someone or some group that hates you, you feel compelled to invent or discover a third way of existence, a way of coexistence.[6]

You engage in compassionate listening when you intentionally tell yourself, "I do not need to be defensive because I have nothing to hide." When you are your authentic self, you no longer need to be competitive because you are invested in peacefully resolving your disputes and improving your relationships. When you use compassionate listening, you are curious and sympathetic. You ask questions to try to clarify your misunderstandings and to understand what the other person is experiencing. You listen to the other person's tale of woe, complaints, or anxiety without chastising them. You let them know you are willing to listen, and then you are attentive because you are friends. Small deeds, such as offering a glass of water or a tissue, have a large impact because they show you are not indifferent to their suffering.

You engage in compassionate speaking when others are distraught. Following are some simple, effective ways to express your concern for others. No mumbling or fidgeting. You don't need long explanations or shoddy excuses; you just need to be forthright, to speak clearly, and to speak from your heart.

- "It's sad that your situation is so difficult. You really do have a mess on your hands."
- "I'm sorry for your loss."
- "I understand that you feel sad."
- "I hear what you are saying."
- "This is a difficult time. I'll stay in touch."
- "I'm sorry this has been such a hard time for you."

Often I tell people, "I'll pray for you." And then they respond by saying, "I appreciate that."

When you see other people for who they are, when you pay attention to their redeeming qualities, when you listen compassionately and have a deeper understanding of their perspective, you defuse your conflicts before they get out of hand. Then you are doing significant damage control.

The Physical Basis of Compassion

Our survival has long depended on understanding what others are doing and feeling. According to an article in the *New York Times* called "Cells That Read Minds," we are physically wired for compassion because of complex cells called mirror neurons, which resonate with the actions and emotions of others. When you see someone pick up a tennis ball, you automatically simulate the same action in your own brain. When you see someone cry, you sense the same feeling within yourself. "Mirror neurons allow us to grasp the minds of others not through conceptual reasoning but through direct simulation. By feeling, not by thinking."[7]

The existence of mirror neurons means we are all subconsciously interconnected, like it or not.

And so our emotions are experienced not merely by ourselves in isolation but also by those around us—both covertly and openly. . . . This interbrain linkage makes bodies move in tandem, thoughts go down the same roads, and emotions run along the same lines. As mirror neurons bridge brains, they create a tacit duet that opens the way for subtle but powerful transactions.[8]

In his book *Social Intelligence*, Daniel Goleman explains that two people can be linked in thoughts, feelings, emotions, and even actions through a neural feedback loop:

A remarkable neural event: the formation between two brains of a functional link, a feedback loop that crosses the skin-and-skull barrier between bodies . . . for the time being forming what amounts to an interbrain circuit. . . . As people loop together, their brains send and receive an ongoing stream of signals that allow them to create a tacit harmony. . . . Looping lets feeling, thought, and actions synchronize. . . . We send and receive internal states for better or worse—whether laughter and tenderness, or tension and rancor. . . . Brains loop outside our awareness, with no special attention or intention demanded.[9]

As we sit down at the bargaining table, we would do well to remember that all human beings are, in fact, connected in myriad ways. When you say to another, "I feel your pain," you aren't kidding!

Questions for Reflection

- Do you have a partner, relative, friend, or coworker in your life who is narcissistic, egotistical, and selfish?
- How has their behavior affected your relationship?
- Have there been times when you believed your interests came first, before you listened carefully to what someone else had to say?
- Do you understand that parenting conflicts and money issues and other disputes require mutual discussion and negotiated agreements in order to obtain closure?
- How often does the matter of "me" versus "we" plague your closest relationships?

Journaling

As you take pen to paper, writing on the topic of selfishness is an "ouch." Let's be real: an element of selfishness is mandatory if you are going to stay alive. As you ponder and answer the preceding questions, keep uppermost in your mind that you are focusing on your clashes, the way you react to your disagreements, the manner in which you communicate and work out your differences, and the ways negotiations collapse when you hoped the outcome would be otherwise. Take the time to write about your experiences with selfish folks and what you have learned, or failed to learn, about conflicted relationships.

Step 5: Be Honest, and Earn the Trust Others Place in You

Foremost, you must understand that you sabotage your relationships when you deceive those you profess to love and/or respect. In the fifth step, you make a promise to yourself that you will act with integrity. Although this step appears to be about your relationships with others, it is really about your relationship with yourself. Ken Keyes devotes a whole section of his book *The Power of Unconditional Love* to advising that you "develop a relationship with yourself before getting deeply involved with somebody else."[10]

I have often wondered why some people find their addiction to lying so enticing. Be cautious of pathological liars because they are not to be trusted today, tomorrow, or ever.

Some people have a tenuous relationship with the truth because they lack confidence in themselves. Some Conflict Avoiders will lie to keep the peace. Some Conflict Goof-Ups are so confused by their own rationalizations that they aren't sure if they are lying or not. Conflict Goof-Ups intentionally misrepresent themselves in sneaky ways to cover up their tracks, hoping they can forestall getting caught, indefinitely. Now is the time to directly address your disturbing issues around deception in order to restore trust again.

Trusting relationships demand honesty, reliability, responsibility, and truth. Inasmuch as our wicked lies destroy our relationships, why do some people feel compelled to damage the trust others should be able to have in them? Strange as it might seem, liars are afraid of the repercussions when the truth is revealed. They don't want to face the music because they hate being grilled about the minute details of their deception, when and where it happened, and why the truth wasn't revealed in the first place. ("When did it happen?" "What were you thinking when you did this?" "Who put you up to it?" "How did you think you could get away with such an atrocity without my knowing?" "Why didn't you tell me sooner?" "How did you get hooked into doing this?" "Who else was involved, and why am I the last to know?") The liar's back is against the wall, and it feels much like being in a courtroom as the questioner is relentless in wanting the whole story.

Generally, we use little white lies because they are an easy way to save face, maintain our dignity, and avoid having to escalate conflict. However, any hint of deception breeds doubt, guardedness, hypervigilance, and mistrust. Nothing is worth breaking someone's trust. There is nagging bitterness and torment when trust is broken.

Author John Amodeo, Ph.D., enlightens our understanding of betrayal:

> Most of us are unprepared to deal with betrayal in a constructive way. Instead, we suppress the pain that it leaves in its wake. We reel in confusion and bitterness, perhaps for

years. We remain numb to our wound and distract ourselves by keeping busy, seeking entertainment, or turning to drugs, alcohol or food. We become turned off to others, concluding that the ill-defined path of love is not for us. We abruptly abandon other people before they have the opportunity to abandon us. We devise cunning methods of getting back at a formerly trusted partner or friend who we believe has wronged us, which may lead to a cycle of mutual vindictiveness that has no winner.[11]

What counts the most in achieving long-lasting, gratifying relationships is being upright, conscientious, and honorable. When your behavior is congruent with your actions, you are direct, steadfast, and forthright. When you speak your truth, you are taking responsibility by being reliable and doing what you promise to do. On the other hand, if your behavior is not consistent with your promises, then your sneakiness is a matter of betrayal and distrust. Talk is cheap if you feign innocence when a lover, a friend, or an employer eventually discovers that you lied. Step 5 takes you on the high road to achieving trustworthy relationships whereby you can relax and enjoy the peace of mind that comes with your telling the truth.

Are You Trustworthy?

Following are several indications that you are *not* being trustworthy:

- You believe you have to resort to force, threats, and coercion to get others to do what you want.
- When there is a problem, you blame and criticize others instead of taking responsibility.
- You tell outright lies to cover up your transgressions.
- You behave in a very defensive way.
- You are power hungry and controlling.

- You take relationships for granted and are not concerned about harming them.
- You quarrel to be the victor, and your relationships go down the drain.

Conflicts can't be resolved when you are secretly telling lies and not admitting to the truth. Mistrust abounds when you don't come clean and admit your transgressions. Mistrust is like a jail sentence, because the deceiver is imprisoned by the fear of being found out. When the betrayer is obliged to face the music, it is a lot worse than the conflict they were trying so hard to avoid.

Let's say your partner confronts you directly and says, "I saw that e-mail you sent. So what's this love note all about?" If you are not trustworthy, you will make up outlandish excuses. Some of us would rather cover up with a comfy blanket of wicked lies rather than 'fess up to our transgressions.

If you have broken someone's trust, begin with step 2, Swallow Your Pride, and Admit Your Mistakes. You rebuild the trust of others when you do the following:

- Offer a heartfelt apology and a plan to make amends.
- Consistently do what you say you are going to do.
- Accept the validity of other points of view.
- Speak openly about your fears, worries, doubts, and vulnerabilities.

How Can You Tell if Someone Else Is Trustworthy?

The matter of who to trust is a tricky one. Some people trust others when they should not, and others are suspicious when it is unjustified. Our early life experiences set the stage for forging trusting relationships. If your childhood caused you to become defensive and suspicious, you must learn to drop your guard, look people in the face, and speak frankly. Then unabashedly, you reveal the best and worst parts of yourself. You are authentic when you have little to hide and present yourself to the world as an honorable person of integrity.

Whenever your conversations with someone else are evasive, most likely he or she is hiding something from you. Take, for example, a husband who arrives home from work quite a bit later than normal, behaving very restlessly. His wife asks, "What's going on? You seem so fidgety." He drops his head and says, "Oh, nothing." She says, "Why didn't you call? I was worried about you." He avoids eye contact and says, "Oh, I was buried in work at the office, and I lost track of time." The pitiful aspect of the wicked lie is that a loved one is suspicious that something is not quite right. He or she becomes wary and apprehensive and fears the worst.

Don't be fooled by those who mislead you. A relationship built on lies is a relationship not worth having. When deceptions are found, and most of them are, there is so much backtracking and forward-reaching work to do to rebuild broken trust.

Questions for Reflection

- Have you ever misbehaved and blamed your naughty conduct on someone else?
- How many times did you say, "I didn't do it," when you know you did?
- How often do you tell little white lies to save face?
- Are you a suspicious person or mostly trusting of others?
- What do you believe is to be gained by being dishonest?
- Do you worry about being found out?
- How do you react when people lie to you?
- What is your understanding of what it takes to restore broken trust?

Journaling

After answering the preceding questions, describe your impressions of trust and mistrust. Inasmuch as this is a difficult topic to address, give yourself time to think about deception. When you lie, what do you lie about? How do you feel about lying? Next, write about how your guilt factors into deception. Then write about how you deal with any shame that you might be feeling. If you are prone to depression and/or anxiety, write about how these emotions feed into your fears of the future. If you have the time, let your thoughts ramble and go back to your early childhood. Write about what your parents had to say about being trustworthy and how they behaved. Wrap up by contrasting your manner of demonstrating your honesty with your family, friends, and colleagues.

Step 6: Never Wave a Red Flag at a Raging Bully

When you take step 6 to heart, you do not quarrel with the Conflict Antagonists of the world, who are everywhere. Bullies like conflict. Because you hate conflict, it is of paramount importance that you understand how they think.

Bullies assume they have the right to do the following:

- Browbeat and oppress you
- Feel superior to you
- Torment and debase you

- Fly off the handle and frighten you
- Throw their weight around
- Get away with all this obnoxious behavior

Bullies have a way of spoiling a perfectly lovely day by creating layers of unnecessary conflict that escalates out of control, especially once you wave a red flag at them. It is your task to be clear that the major problem with bullies is that they are insufferable. Understand that bullies feel justified in oppressing you because you are too scared to confront them.

The "Stop!" Strategy

I recommend the "Stop!" strategy anytime you are flushed with heated anger. This strategy is simple and instantly effective. All you do is firmly say, "Stop!" to your Conflict Antagonist. If the other person presses on, then loudly and firmly say, "Stop!" Repeat, "Stop!" a third or fourth time, if necessary.

There is nothing wrong with saying, "Stop!" You will never regret saying it later on. It is not offensive to the other person, so it does not up the ante in your discussion. Often the other person is so surprised they stop escalating the argument right away. I tell my clients, "Imagine you are driving and you see a green traffic light. Before you get to the intersection, the light turns to yellow. And because you're going too fast, you have to put on the brakes and come to screeching stop before the traffic light turns red. If you keep driving, you'll run the red light and in all likelihood hurt yourself or someone else."

The "Stop!" strategy was a must for Mark and me because it gave us time to shift gears and realize that whatever we were arguing about was not really important. So we were serious when we said, "Stop!" When one of us used the word, we dropped our argument like a hot potato and found better ways to spend our time.

The "Stop!" strategy is mandatory for anyone who has ever argued and walked away enraged. Using this technique, you put a stop to the uproar and turmoil when it gets out of hand. When you firmly say, "Stop!" you are taking back your power and investing your angry energy in doing significant damage control. After saying, "Stop!" you may be able to negotiate in a reasonable manner, or you may decide to walk away and take a break.

Other Phrases to Use

Bullies guess that you won't stand up to them or speak your mind. You might even hide out someplace or run away. They might anticipate with glee that you will retaliate, because they don't mind fighting. Do not be tempted to engage in such absurd eye-for-an-eye thinking, for it saps your energy time and again.

Following are short, polite statements designed to stop your arguments on the spot:

- "I'm not arguing anymore."
- "If you want to argue, you'll have to argue with yourself."
- "I'm sick and tired of arguing, and I don't want to be mad at you."
- "I refuse to argue because it's a pointless waste of time."
- "I have better things to do than argue."
- "I love you, so let's not ruin our relationship by arguing about stupid stuff."

The following retorts work best when they are firmly spoken immediately after a loved one or coworker has been harsh, rude, inappropriate, or obstinate. If you hope to have enduring relationships that make you feel proud to be who you are, it makes sense to calmly and politely take the wind out of your tyrant's sails by standing firm and saying:

- "I've had enough of your barking at me!"
- "I can't stand your being so mean. It makes me feel like two cents."
- "It is time for us to put on the brakes and do it right instead of torturing each other."
- "Let's be grown-up enough to stop criticizing each other."
- "I'm not hiding from my truth so I would appreciate your being honest with me."
- "I can't play ostrich anymore, so please tell me what's on your mind."
- "I know I am anal retentive, so get me the information on time and I won't badger you anymore."
- "I admit I'm indecisive. Just give me a little more time to figure out what I want to do next."

These brief statements give big bullies time to consider changing their behavior. This is how you set limits to what you will or will not tolerate.

- "I'm not intimidated by your trying to persecute me, so don't bother to blow your bullish horn at me!"
- "Go bully yourself, because I don't want any part of your manipulative threats."
- "I don't need any more conflict, so stop harassing me. This is getting ridiculous!"
- "I'm not putting up with your tormenting ways, so back off and behave yourself."

Having lived for twenty-five years in a physically abusive marriage that did vast harm to our children, it was imperative that I protect my youngsters and myself as best as I could. These were the days before battering was a household word. At that time in my life, I wouldn't dare confront my husband for fear that he would inflict even more violence on the children and me. Secretly I worried that he might kill us! So be aware that it's vitally important to protect your kids and yourself first, not last.

Questions for Reflection

- How difficult is it for you to admit your mistakes?
- Do any of your family members or coworkers refuse to admit that they are wrong?
- Are you prone to making snap judgments about others?
- How important is saving face to you?
- Are you usually accommodating or defensive?
- Would you say that you are trustworthy?
- Do you feel entitled to lie often or rarely?
- How often do you praise or encourage others?
- How does it feel to be praised or encouraged by someone important to you?
- What is your usual response to a compliment?
- How often do you laugh about your controversial issues in your primary relationships?

Journaling

Answering the preceding questions will give you much food for thought. Write about your experiences with making mistakes.

Now write about the people who have been dishonest with you or who have betrayed you. Be mindful of your emotions—whether you feel sad, glad, mad, and/or scared. Also write about the good and bad times you have had with loved ones, friends, and coworkers.

Next, describe how you encourage loved ones and coworkers. Also describe how you feel when others praise you.

Write about some of the times you have laughed when your relationships were conflicted. Describe a funny experience you had recently with someone meaningful to you. Recall a time in the past or present when you have felt relieved, uplifted, and joyous.

Keep in mind to be thankful every day for what you have. Write a few lines about the importance of gratitude.

Step 7: Use Encouragement and Laughter to Keep Conflict at Bay

Former president Gerald Ford often would tell his friends, "You can disagree without being disagreeable." Conflict can be minimized when we accentuate the positive, take a friendly outlook, and treat others with approval.

Our hunger for encouragement starts when we are infants. Our parents, grandparents, and caregivers said, "Patty-cake, patty-cake," and with encouragement we learned to say the words.

Our parents got all excited as they laughed, and, as little tots, we were all smiles. These are precious moments to be remembered. Encouragement nourishes other people's creative endeavors and lets them know we care about them. By encouraging others, we know we are helping them to achieve their goals. As we see them thrive, we are happy for them.

We all want to be supported and not rejected. We seek approval, and we want to be treated courteously. Kind words of validation lift our spirits because we know our loved ones care about us. Another's support is invaluable in reaffirming our self-worth—and surely, we all need a boatload of that. We can and do change for the better when we are energized to believe that we will accomplish our goals.

As you support others, they reciprocate in kind. By validating your loved ones, you enhance the well-being of your close connections. And as others encourage you, then you feel more confident. Indeed, healthy relationships generally thrive on unspoken reciprocal agreements.

Encouragement reduces conflict between partners, siblings, parents, children, and peers in amazing ways. No one is so self-assured that they cannot benefit from the support of others. The following words of support, praise, and encouragement will be a gift to others so they have good reason to believe in themselves:

- "Wow, you did it!"
- "You are amazing; I know you can handle this conflict."
- "I'm so proud of you."
- "You are smart; I know you will figure it out."
- "I am so glad you are my friend."
- "What a blessing you are to me."
- "You have been wonderful to me."
- "I trust your judgment."
- "I have confidence that you will do well."
- "You are a beautiful person inside and out."

- "I feel fortunate to know someone as caring as you."
- "You are important to me. Thank you for being just who you are."
- "I appreciate your support; you are always there when I need you."
- "I want you to know how much I value our friendship."

Encouragement and praise are meant to nourish your creative self and inspire you to accomplish your dreams. As you support your loved ones, then mutually, they also care about you. As you see others succeed, you treasure the warmth of their friendship.

When other people encourage us, then we are inspired to persevere and accomplish our goals. Mark would often say, "Nothing we do is ever wasted." So many times this special message has proved to be true for me.

When Mark was ten years old, his mother gave him this challenging message: "You can do anything you aspire to do, if you set your mind to it!" He was so encouraged by his mother's words that he gave this message to our children, his employees, and his many friends, and now these same words are handed down to our grandchildren and all who will benefit from his caring support.

Carole, one of Mark's employees, told me how much she profited from his praise and encouragement. She said, "Mark had the remarkable ability to see through me; he saw the qualities and attributes that I was unable, even unwilling, to recognize. Then he would sit back and watch as time after time I would come to realize my own capacities. When I accomplished a difficult task, Mark would laugh and I would sheepishly agree that he had been right all along. He was patient enough to let me come to these insights on my own, one at a time."

As for laughter—well, there is nothing funny about conflict unless you make a concerted effort to see the ludicrous side of your disputes. Life can be tedious, and if you take to heart every word and deed that rubs you the wrong way, you are going to be hard-pressed to get along with others, because you cannot change their inane idiosyncrasies. If you are going to resolve your disputes in a world filled with contentious people, then being able to laugh at yourself is the best elixir I know for disposing of conflict.

Let's not forget that each person has his or her unique character traits, quirks, foibles, and foolishness that might seem crazy to another. So it behooves us to give other people some slack. If you're not so hard on them, they might be more forgiving of your eccentricities. And remember that when you focus on another's strengths, you have a different viewpoint. Now don't hold your breath, but sometimes others will also reciprocate in kind.

Laugh Our Conflicts Away

Our ability to see life whimsically is one of the safest ways to defuse conflict. Laughter makes our conflicts seem less menacing and dramatically changes our perspective. Seeing the funny side of conflicts allows us to be in touch with the worst and best aspects of our relationships. Laughter is a healthy way to offset our daily frustrations and suffering. Saying something funny relieves worry and distress. Personally, I enjoy laughing especially when I'm tired and worn out because laughter lifts my spirits and brightens my day. Laughter might even save our sanity. When we laugh 'til it hurts, our disagreements don't seem as important.

Many good people are so deadly serious. They work hard, grit their teeth, and worry. Usually, they are weary and in no mood to deal with conflict. They might protest that they aren't depressed, but they don't smile and they aren't having any fun. Without laughter, life becomes tedious and dreary.

Humor is a valuable remedy when your conflicts are not immediately fixable. Diane and Otto had been married twenty-eight years when they separated for a year. The couple had a long struggle to restore trust after Otto confessed that he had considered having an affair with Diane's best friend. Although Diane did not condone Otto's behavior, she could understand his reasons for being unfaithful, and she was relieved he had cut off the relationship before it had gone any further. Diane and Otto were growing closer, and they hoped to move back in together in the near future.

Diane had a twinkle in her eye when she said, "Otto and I have this deep grief because we are not able to be perfect."

Otto feigned a pompous attitude and said, "To think that I might have any character flaws!"

The three of us had a good belly laugh because unabashedly, each partner was speaking their truth. I said, "Your humor makes the intolerable tolerable, and in authentic ways you are regaining trust in each other."

In his book *Grow Up!: How Taking Responsibility Can Make You a Happy Adult*, esteemed marriage and family therapist Frank Pittman describes how he and his sister found humor in their difficult relationship with their alcoholic mother:

> Parents who were clearly imperfect can be helpful to you. While you were trying to grow up despite their fumbling efforts, you had to develop skills and tolerances other kids did not. Some of the strongest people I know grew up taking care of inept, invalid, or psychotic parents—but they knew their parents were not normal, healthy, and whole. Children of imperfect parents might be grateful to their imperfect parents for the opportunities to develop unexpected strengths. My sister and I are firmly convinced that our mother's alcoholism made us stronger people and better caretakers. Such a tragicomic existence certainly did wonders for our sense of humor.[12]

I suggest laughing 'til it hurts when your disputes are going nowhere. Mark had me in stitches with his ridiculous remarks. One day he said, "Lee, I have a wonderful title for your next book: *Arguing for a Successful Marriage: Getting the Most from Your Disputes.*" This was truly prophetic, considering that Mark died two and a half years before I thought about writing this book.

On a bad day, seeing the humor in opposing points of view is a refreshing way to shift your perspective so you see the tragedy as well as the comedy. Some of your disagreements are so outrageous that laughter can be the remedy that lightens your heart. A funny joke can easily shift your mood and often dispense with whatever was troubling you.

Office Visit: Carol and Andrew

I had a conversation with my longtime friend Andrew, a well-known physician, and his wife, Carol. Andrew said, "I hate conflict because it creates a very uncomfortable visceral reaction in the pit of my stomach and a more rapid heartbeat that is very uncomfortable. You see, when I was growing up, my dad and sister screamed at the top of their lungs, every day. I couldn't bear their vicious arguments, so I decided the best I could do was defuse any conflicted situation with humor. I found out that I could make others laugh and I became expert at it. This makes it possible for me to walk away from hostile situations."

Carol told me, "You know no one is perfect, but basically Andrew and I get along so well because we are reasonable, we can talk. We usually don't get ticked off, because we love each other. We have six grandchildren, and Andrew and I take life as it comes. Best of all, we laugh. We know there will be difficult times, but our determination to have fun and enjoy each day is our salvation."

I told them, "Andrew and Carol, you are expert Conflict Innovators. You honor and respect one another; you make a habit of sharing jokes, and you are happy because you appreciate each other and never take your life or your relationship for granted."

My client Rosemary had a story to tell me about her cantankerous brothers, Stanley and Joel. Rosemary said, "I'm heartbroken because every year on Christmas day our family of twenty-two relatives gets together to celebrate. But I'm already upset and I'm furious when I think about how my brothers insist on arguing. They have never gotten along. They criticize each other, bring up old conflicts, and make nasty remarks until it gets to be an ugly scene. Nobody in our family will ever confront them, so inevitably, our Christmas is ruined.

"Usually, Stanley starts the bickering, and Joel jumps in and ups the ante. I can tell that the rest of our family is unhappy, judging by their faces. What a farce our Christmas celebration is! I hate to see our family get-together spoiled every year. What can I do to stop this fiasco?"

I said, "Rosemary, you really do have an unruly situation on your hands. Stanley and Joel are Conflict Antagonists who are instigating needless mayhem. I think it's best to use your anger in a constructive way. I suggest that you arrange to speak to Stanley and Joel together. Be sure to meet them face-to-face. Say something like, 'Now that Christmas is coming up, I want you to know that your arguments are disruptive to our family members, who come a great distance to celebrate this holiday. It is disrespectful to make everyone else miserable. So I would appreciate it if you would not pick a fight with each other. Then our whole family will have a memorable and peaceful time to enjoy ourselves.' You might also say something to encourage them, such as, 'I have confidence that you both will be able to control yourselves.'"

Rosemary said, "You know, I hate conflict, so I'll probably be shaking in my boots when I say this to my brothers. But this strategy makes sense to me, so I'll do it."

When we met after Christmas, Rosemary said, "I wasn't sure what Stanley and Joel would say when I confronted them. Actually, they were dumbfounded that I had the nerve to speak up. I could tell that Stanley was peeved, but he managed to hold his tongue because he must have been numb with shock. As for Joel, he was as quiet as a mouse.

"When Christmas came, I just reminded them about our conversation. Stanley started to get cranky about the dog being in the way, and I quickly turned the situation into a joke. Fortunately, the dog was a good distraction—we put antlers on his head, which was pretty funny. During the Christmas celebration, I privately told Stanley and Joel individually that this was the best Christmas we had ever had, and our entire family had a wonderful time."

We each live on God's time. As we are mortal, it is important to bless each day and be grateful to be alive. Ultimately, we get some of our needs met, but not all of them, because conflicts have a way of intruding when you least expect them. On the other hand, goodly doses of laughter make it all worthwhile as you count your blessings.

Questions for Reflection

- How often do you praise or encourage others?
- How do you feel when you praise or encourage others?
- How does it feel to be praised or encouraged by someone important to you?
- What is your usual response to a compliment?
- How often do you laugh about your controversial issues?

Journaling

Answer the preceding questions, and then take five or ten minutes to write about your experiences with encouraging others. Then describe how you have been encouraged by your loved ones and coworkers. Next, write down some of the times you laughed when your relationships were conflicted. Be mindful of your emotions—whether you feel sad, glad, mad, or scared. Take another two minutes to describe a funny experience you had recently.

7

Twenty Core Truths to Help Your Conversations

I am delighted to share with you my twenty core truths. These are my favorite observations about conflict, relationships, and human nature. Remembering these twenty core truths will help you as you bravely take a position and address the conflicted areas of your life that need attention.

Core Truth #1: Two People Relate to Each Other Four Ways and More

When couples or families come to my office, one of my first tasks is to explain the complexity of communication, which is best understood when you take into account this core premise: two people relate to each other four ways and more. A conversation is more than a two-way street. Imagine four streets that are all full of traffic at the same time. The four ways in this core truth come from the fact that when I relate to you, I am also relating to myself, and when you relate to me, you are also relating to yourself.

For example, my client Lakeisha took her daughter Shandi to Take Our Daughters to Work Day at her office. Lakeisha was thrilled to show her daughter what she did all day. However, her conversation was taking place on at least two levels. On the surface, she was relating to Shandi, explaining to her the duties of her job. At the same time, Lakeisha also was relating to her younger self. She remembered herself at Shandi's age, as a kid who wished her mother had a real job. Shandi, on the other hand, grew up with a working mother. Her younger self wished she had a mother who didn't have to work at all.

Three people relate to each other nine ways, and four people interact sixteen ways with one another. Thus, the *more* people involved, the *more* their interactions multiply exponentially, which is reason enough for opposing points of view to erupt like wildfire.

Core Truth #2: People Assume They Are Right Until They Admit They Are Wrong

When you disagree with someone, you are likely to get into a power struggle. Ever since the dawn of history, wars have been fought to decide which side is right and which side is wrong, and each side thinks, "God is on our side."

The issue of who is right and who is wrong is in the eye of the beholder. We make snap decisions and are absolutely convinced we are correct. That means the other person is automatically wrong. Generally, we feel entitled to be right because we believe in the value of how we perceive our clashes. Bypassing the whole issue of whether or not we are actually correct, we jump straight to making accusations and defending our position. We get annoyed and dig in our heels. We might even lie to bolster our position. It isn't convenient to acknowledge that we might be partially right and partially wrong. We certainly aren't thinking that there might be evidence indicating both sides are partially right or both sides are entirely wrong. Having assumed we are right, we stick to our guns until we willingly or under duress admit we made a mistake.

I have learned that it is easy to make a mistake and assume that I'm right, only to find out after the fact how wrong I was.

Core Truth #3: You Are the Center of Your World, but You Are Not the Center of the Universe

By this I mean that we are a world unto ourselves, but we must acknowledge that there are other universes out there. When we think only about ourselves, we see no shades of gray. We become rigid and inflexible because our way is the only way. This kind of polarized thinking accelerates conflict to dizzying proportions. A self-centered stance refutes the basic need for compromise and cooperative teamwork.

As established earlier, we need to be a little bit selfish just to make sure we meet our basic needs. Even Mother Teresa had to eat. But egocentrism is carried to an extreme when we are power hungry and have a self-centered mind-set.

Have you ever noticed that people who are relentlessly self-absorbed are exhausting to be around? Daniel Goleman describes the narcissist as follows:

> The narcissist's sense of entitlement endows him with the feeling that ordinary rules and boundaries do not apply to him. . . . A blunted empathy, remember, stands high on the list of traits of the narcissist, along with an exploitative attitude and vain self-centeredness.[1]

When we are self-absorbed, we have little or no tolerance for dealing with controversy. Egocentrism offers no remedies for resolving conflict, as selfishness is accompanied by a sense of entitlement: "I deserve to be on the receiving end, and I do not need to even think about giving recognition or appreciation to all the people who have given their time and energy on my behalf."

Wake up and realize that others see their world differently than you do. Take off your blinders and look at your options, and then keep in mind the merit of cooperation and compromise when it comes to resolving your conflicts. When you acknowledge that there are other universes out there, you experience the joy of putting another's needs ahead of your own.

Core Truth #4: Believing You Are a Victim Makes You One

Attachment theory started with analyzing the relationships between children and their parents/caregivers. When attachment theory was extended to include adult romantic relationships, four styles of attachment were identified:

1. Secure
2. Anxious-preoccupied
3. Dismissive-avoidant
4. Fearful-avoidant

Securely attached people tend to be enthusiastic about themselves and their partners. Statistics indicate that 55 percent of the people in the United States feel comfortable and at ease in getting close to others. They are readily accessible, have good intentions, and tend to be intimate and trusting with others.

Anxious-preoccupied people are clingy and worried about their relationships. They value intimacy but tend to have low self-esteem.

Dismissive-avoidant people value their independence, which may translate into a tendency to avoid intimate relationships.

Fearful-avoidant people would like to have close relationships, but they find it too difficult to trust others. They tend to have low self-esteem and to feel unworthy.

As you can see from these descriptions, people with low self-esteem have trouble with their romantic relationships because they can't believe anyone could really love them. They tend to need reassurance that their partner is loyal. They are hungry for love, warmth, and caring, but when they take the attitude that life shouldn't be too good, they often end up reaping what they sow. They can be hypervigilant, self-conscious, and jealous and thus inadvertently drive their partners away.[2]

When we live and breathe the victim mentality, we feel deprived, as if we didn't get our just due. We feel discouraged when another is disapproving. We feel guilty when we are censured because we have not lived up to another's expectations. Victims are trapped in a maze of inner conflict because they doubt themselves and blame the people who have wounded them.

Victims harbor the following pessimistic thoughts:

- "Life shouldn't be too good."
- "I don't deserve the best."
- "If they really knew me, they wouldn't like me."
- "I am a bad person."
- "Nothing I do is ever good enough."
- "I can't do anything right."
- "Pity me. I'm a lost soul, and there's nothing I can do about it!"

The victims' way of thinking is distorted because their early childhood script is a negative one. They may have been treated harshly or repeatedly reminded of their worthlessness. It's nearly impossible for them to grow into confident, self-assured, successful adults when all their young lives there were people telling them that they would never amount to anything. Some victims can't stand success because they don't value themselves.

We cannot alter our past, but we are capable of believing that we are lovable, valuable, and worthy. Many of us of have strengths and talents that we have not yet fully realized.

Strategically, I suggest to my victim clients that they take a time-out once or twice a day to feel sorry for themselves, from five to thirty minutes per day as needed. They can cry or pamper themselves and not feel guilty about doing so. The results are excellent, because then they have the energy to get on with their life without being burdened down with unwarranted depressing thoughts.

Martyrs

Martyrs are ambitious victims. They usually are the Conflict Fixers who are the do-gooders of the world. Martyrs are competitive workaholics who believe that no one can do as much as they do. On the job, martyrs work overtime and don't get paid as much as they deserve. Family-wise, no one else can match their industrious output. Martyrs are the sacrificial lambs who suffer in silence and carry a grudge for years on end. I've noticed that martyrs play the "good person" role by being willing victims who suffer for a cause. They wear themselves to a frazzle as they put in a lot of time and energy supporting worthy community causes. In fact, their family is often neglected, and they overextend themselves at the expense of their own health.

Martyrs test the limits of their endurance as self-sacrifice comes first, not last. Then they complain about how much they have sacrificed. The problem is, no one asked them to go to such lengths. If all this seems paradoxical—well, I'm here to tell you that the martyr role is indeed a common one. In fact, I played it for many years.

Essentially, martyrs need to rethink how they can establish a more equitable workload at home, on the job, and on behalf of the community so they can have gratifying relationships.

Pessimists

When we harbor negative thoughts—"I can't please her because no matter what I do, it isn't right." "I'm frustrated because he thinks I'm not good enough and then I start to believe it." "What's the use of trying? I goof up, she gets mad, and our relationship deteriorates."—then we reinforce a sense of futility and despair. Pessimists automatically imagine the worst is happening: a loved one is in deep trouble, a parent is very ill, a friend has had a horrible accident. We usually take our pessimistic notions seriously, and what a relief it is to discover that our negative thoughts were actually wrong.

Take note: our attitudes are contagious and rub off on others. We can choose the dark despair of pessimism or an optimistic, life-affirming attitude that offers us hope. In any negotiation, we must stay on the positive side or we are lost in an untidy heap of negativity.

Now is the time to monitor your pessimistic way of thinking. Each time you recognize a negative thought, quickly replace it by putting a positive thought in your head. When you shift to the optimistic side, your relationships improve. If you remain on the negative side, it leads to disillusionment and unhappy relationships.

If you are experiencing a dark period in your life, there is no need to adopt a pessimistic point of view. The law of physics confirms that there is one absolute constant, and that is change. There is an ebb and flow in life, because nothing stays the same. Remind yourself that there is balance in the universe, and eventually things will change.

Core Truth #5: You Can Think and Feel at the Same Time

OK, this core truth may sound like a blinding flash of the obvious, but when we are in the middle of a dispute, we don't always take advantage of both our heads and our hearts. Sometimes we are so busy building a flawless logical argument that we forget to notice our feelings. Other times we are so caught up in our anger or fear that we forget to use rational thought. In general, men tend to think before feeling, and women tend to feel before thinking. Remember to think about what you are feeling and to feel what you are thinking.

Core Truth #6: Generally, Most Men Like to Fix Mechanical Things; Most Women Want to Fix Relationships

I understand this core truth uses stereotypes, so before you get upset with me, let me say I know many women who fix mechanical things and many men who fix relationships. However, I have also had many experiences with couples in my office who play directly to stereotype. Here is an example:

Alexandra says, "Patrick, I want very much to talk to you about our future. Our thirty-five-week anniversary is coming up!"

He says, "I thought we'd been dating for, like, a few months."

She says, "I'm worried about where we are headed. I mean, I need to know how serious this relationship is."

He examines his keys.

She says, "Whenever I try to talk to you, you go in the garage and start working on your car. Why do you care so much about that car, anyway?"

He looks amazed.

I make a suggestion. "Patrick, would you be willing to let Alexandra help you work on your car?"

He looks skeptical but says, "Sure, we can try that, if she wants to do it."

It is very common for women to get to a point in a relationship where they need assurances about what happens next. In my experience, many men are happy to just passively go along the way things are. When the women begin to ask pointed questions about the relationship, the men develop a sudden interest in fixing the car or repairing the lawn mower. Understanding this core truth should help both to better understand where the other is coming from.

Core Truth #7: Communication Is Not the Same as Conversation

I think people enjoy talking to their dogs because their dogs can't talk back. The dog repertoire is pretty much limited to approval. A conversation requires give-and-take, and having conversations is essential to preventing conflict. As a result, it's important to understand the differences between communication and real conversation.

- The best communication is a face-to-face conversation, where the people involved are able to shake hands and to read each other's nonverbal clues and body language. This is why I will fly across the country, if need be, to meet someone important or to have an important conversation.
- The next best communication is a phone call, where you are able to provide feedback and responses back and forth. Although you are not in the presence of the other person, his or her comments and timbre of voice are very informative.
- A letter or an e-mail counts as communication but not as conversation. Although you may be expecting an answer eventually, a letter or an e-mail is basically a one-sided effort.
- An instant message or text message hardly counts as communication at all, no matter how many emoticons you add.
- Communicating through third parties should be illegal. Kidding aside, involving meddlers (see Chapter 2) guarantees that your message will be distorted and corrupted.

Core Truth #8: Polarized, Black-and-White Thinking Is a Trap

There are no absolutes other than the one god, life, and death. Everything else is gray.Polarized thinking speaks to inaccurate absolutes—right or wrong, all or nothing. Relationships are either catastrophic or amenable, with nothing in between. Conversations are clumsy or rewarding. Polarized thinkers tend to think in terms of always or never, disappointing or gratifying, and loving or hating.

Author John Amodeo addresses the difficulties of a polarized stance:

> We demonstrate a self-righteous reactivity when life fails to gratify us. We speak in absolutes and think in simplistic categories of black or white, good or bad. "You're either for me or against me! Either you love me or you don't." We have little patience to discern fine shades of meaning and little tolerance for personal differences with others. Life is experienced as a competition or battle. The goal is being right and winning, or, at least, surviving.[3]

Doris and Betty were blinded as they exaggerated their complaints with "always" and "never" statements:

Doris: "I'm discouraged because I see so little of my daughter, Betty. She's *always* so distant, and she *never* acts like she wants to be friends."

Betty: "I'm irritated with my mother, Doris, because she's overbearing and intrusive. She *never* approves of how I raise my children."

Doris: "You *never* visit me anymore; you're *always* too busy."

Betty: "You *always* have to be right."

Doris: "You *never* listen to what I have to say."

Betty: "You *always* are so picky, and that's not how I am."

This conversation, so permeated with absolutes, became more and more pessimistic. Neither mother nor daughter understood that speaking in softer terms would at least crack open the door to reconciliation and mutual understanding.

Polarized, black-and-white thinking means that your interpretation of what another person said is the opposite of what you had in mind. When you don't listen carefully to *how* you speak, you don't notice that your thoughts are focused on *me* to the exclusion of *we*. When we are narrow-minded and inflexible, we don't see the shades of gray, and we make it impossible to have realistic, successful discussions.

Core Truth #9: Written Agreements Are Powerful

In my experience, both men and women will generally honor the written word. In my practice, I encourage the use of contracts to formalize a verbal agreement. This agreement usually has to do with either of the following:

- The way you are going to conduct your discussion (for example, "I agree to be truthful")
- The way you have concluded your discussion (for example, "I will take out the trash on Thursday nights")

Write out your agreement, date it, and have both parties sign it. This is a nice way to honor the work you have done together, as well as to ensure there are no misunderstandings in the future.

If you are preparing to have a serious discussion, I highly advise reviewing Chapter 6, "The Seven Essential Steps to Managing Conflict Constructively," and making a written agreement to follow them. You could make an agreement with yourself, as a reminder, or a mutual agreement with someone else, to establish ground rules for your conversation.

Signing your name to a document is not something people take lightly. Agreements that are written up and signed are more powerful and have more long-lasting results than less formal arrangements.

Core Truth #10: Failure Is a Learning Opportunity, Not a Time to Give Up and Stop Seeking a Creative Solution

Good things can take time—a long time! If you tried once or twice to solve your conflict without success, this does not mean you are doomed to fail. Anything important is worth pursuing—multiple times, if necessary. If you give up, you are really just demonstrating lack of ingenuity.

There's a great deal of folk wisdom on the subject of failure, probably because it is such a common experience. Failure is always a learning opportunity. In her *Well-Being Newsletter*, therapist Amy Sprague Champeau writes:

> Don't be afraid to make a mistake. Give yourself lots of permission to try. There is no failure in creativity. Why not be free to make plenty of "mistakes"? They may not end up being "mistakes" at all![4]

In *The Search for Existential Identity*, psychologist, James F. T. Bugental, Ph.D., describes his innovative manner of seeking new ideas:

> First, I kind of "soak in" the issues for quite a while. I let all angles of it hit me, and I experience the anxiety, anger, tension, or whatever emotions go with it. But I don't, if I can help it, try to solve it right away. Then, when the process is working best, I talk to someone. . . . And all I do when I talk is say whatever comes to me about the matter I'm concerned with—what it feels like and how blocked I feel and whatever else comes to mind about it. And the person I'm talking with just helps me say it all out and avoids advising, criticizing, or

getting in my way. At this point, an interesting thing begins
to happen. As I open myself inside so that I say whatever
comes to mind, all sorts of new perspectives open up also.
What seemed a hopeless situation gradually comes to have
other possibilities.[5]

There are many creative ideas for approaching, and reapproach-
ing, your disputes until you find a way that works. If at first you
don't succeed, try, try again.

Core Truth #11: The Almighty Gave Us the Capacity to Laugh at Our Foibles So We Would Not Get Bored with Our Relationships

Well, this core truth is self-explanatory!

I mentioned in Chapter 6 that using encouragement and laughter keep conflict at bay (this is the last of the seven steps). When
emotions are running high, people actually appreciate some humor
to uplift our spirits.

People often say that laughter "bubbles." Without bubbles,
champagne would be grape juice and bread would be cement.
Without laughter, our relationships would be equally flat and
heavy. A mutually appreciated sense of humor will keep a close
relationship sparkling for many years.

Daniel Goleman refers to the "happy face advantage":

Smiles have an edge over all other emotional expression: the
human brain prefers happy faces, recognizing them more

readily and quickly than those with negative expressions. . . . Some neuroscientists suggest that the brain has a system for positive feelings that stays primed for activity, causing people to be in upbeat moods more often than negative and to have a more positive outlook on life. . . . Indeed, laughter may be the shortest distance between two brains, an unstoppable infectious spread that builds an instant social bond.[6]

Core Truth #12: If You Want People to Love You, Then You Be the Leader and Love Them First

I have counseled many couples who found themselves at a hostile impasse, each person too hurt to be the first to make a conciliatory gesture. This stalemate can go on forever, sometimes until death makes reconciliation impossible.

Once I overheard a mother in a café talking to a friend. Tears were running down her cheeks as she described her estrangement from her daughter, with whom she had not spoken in three years. It would have been highly inappropriate for me to go over to her table, but even knowing this, it took all of my self-restraint not to say, "You have already lost three years of your daughter's life. You must make the first move. Call her *today!*"

When Yvonne first came to see me, she said, "For the past three years, I've had a terrible relationship with my daughter, Lori. We don't get along. We quarrel, she gets mad at me, and then I'm furious with her. Lori is twenty-six years old, and she's driving me crazy. She phones every day complaining about whatever I did wrong. Usually she's in a bitchy mood and I get sucked into arguing with her. Then she hangs up the phone and I'm a wreck!"

On a hunch, I asked Yvonne if she was critical of Lori. Yvonne looked surprised and asked, "How did you know that?"

I said, "Just a hunch. I know that mothers commonly criticize their daughters. That seems to be important to them, but they usually overstep their boundaries."

Yvonne said, "Honestly, Lori and I are constantly criticizing each other. She knows how to push my buttons! I know it's a tall order, but what I would like is a peaceful relationship with my daughter."

I said, "Yvonne, you are a well-meaning Conflict Fixer, but you must stop your criticisms and instead use words of encouragement. Lori needs to know that you approve of her. By praising her and giving her lots of validation, you show your love for her. Lori wants to know that you like her just the way she is. She wants to know that you appreciate her many talents. She wants to know that you admire her for what she accomplishes."

Three weeks later I met Yvonne again, and she had a big grin on her face. She said, "I did what you told me to do, and I'm happy to say it made a big difference. Now that we don't criticize each other, we have no more arguments, and Lori and I are getting along fine. Now I'm at peace with her."

I asked Yvonne to explain how her relationship with Lori improved so quickly. She told me, "Well, I started to be supportive. She would still be critical and cranky, but I listened to her complaints, and I said, 'I hear you.' I didn't correct her."

I asked Yvonne if she would be willing to give me the specific words of encouragement that she said to Lori. Here they are verbatim:

"That's great!"
"I'm sure you'll choose the right way."
"Good idea."

"Sounds like you're on the ball."

"I know you can do it!"

I said, "Yvonne, you did it just right. This is great! You were enthusiastic and sincere with your encouraging words. Now Lori knows you believe in her. This is the way she learns to trust her own judgment. By strengthening your bond with your daughter, you get to be best friends."

Yvonne replied, "I was so intent on mothering Lori by telling her what to do and how to act that it never occurred to me that I was smothering her and making both of us feel wretched."

I said, "I appreciate your sharing this story because validation, support, and encouragement are what we all need in order to thrive."

Yvonne said, "Thank you, I appreciate your help. Now I'm wondering how I ever thought I could *fix* Lori when I can barely *fix* myself?" And with that we both had a good laugh!

Core Truth #13: People Are Doing the Best They Can at Any Given Time, and if They Knew Better, They Might Consider Doing Better

I have a pet peeve. I dislike the word *dysfunctional*. These days it is a buzzword of sorts—"my family was dysfunctional," "their relationship is dysfunctional," and so on.

It's true that family dynamics can be dysfunctional. We can look back fifteen years and realize our family was in chaos. We can look down the street and determine that another family is having problems. But for the people actually living through the situation, this is their life. In all likelihood they are miserable. If they knew any better, they would do better. They don't know how.

Let's all avoid judgmental words like *dysfunctional* and extend acceptance to others (and ourselves) when trapped in conflicted situations because they (or we) don't know any better.

Core Truth #14: Regrettably, Perfection Is a Wish, Not a Reality

I'll let you in on a secret. Not all of the advice in this book is wholly original. In fact, some of the commonsense recommendations in these chapters have been effectively used for centuries by people coping with conflict. The irony is that we have to keep reminding ourselves of the same truths over and over again, because we never get things quite right. Reality is always a work in progress. All the wisdom of all the books in the world have not managed to help people deal with conflict effectively, so I am trying a new approach, in my own way, and hoping it will make a difference. Perhaps my voice will be heard where others were not.

By the way, I guarantee all of the advice in this book is tried and true. If you add my years of life experience and years of clinical experience together, you get more than a century of wisdom. I hope you find it helpful.

Core Truth #15: Trial and Error Is Tantamount to Fake It 'til You Make It

A wise therapist once said, "Emotions are the tail over the fence." I thought this was brilliant, so I shared it with one of my clients the next day. He had absolutely no idea what I was talking about.

Sometimes it is beneficial to change our actions, routines, and behavior first and wait for the emotional changes to settle in later. The horse going over the fence is our actions, and the horse's tail is our emotions.

There are so many situations when it makes sense to leap first. Here are a few:

- You behave lovingly toward your partner first and find this changes the relationship so much that in a short while you actually feel more loving.
- You speak in front of a crowd, find out that it isn't so bad, and eventually are so comfortable with public speaking that you become a famous lecturer.
- You hate exercise, but you sign up for yoga, drag your body to the gym once a week, and after two months can't wait for class.
- You sign up for an art class, tell yourself you are an artist, and in time actually become one.

Trial and error is another way of staying creative after your two, ten, or twenty approaches to resolving your conflicts happen to fail. "Fake it 'til you make it" isn't actually about being fake. It's about getting real.

Core Truth #16: Reality Is in the Eye of the Beholder, Which Makes It Difficult to Distinguish Common Sense from Crazy-Making

Each individual has a separate viewpoint or scenario that is valid for that person. As we've already seen, people assume their viewpoint is correct until they are obliged to see otherwise. Conflict is caused by mutual failure to acknowledge the validity of another person's viewpoint or scenario. Unless people are able to find common ground, they are likely to get defensive. This explains how thorny conflicts quickly get out of hand when people quarrel. Efforts to communicate, confront, and negotiate come to a standstill when we cannot get past accepting our individual differences with any degree of reverence and insight.

There are some sound reasons why understanding conflict can seem so elusive. The book *Getting to Yes: Negotiating Agreement Without Giving In* gives us a realistic appraisal of how to deal with conflict:

> Understanding the other side's thinking is not simply a useful activity that will help you solve your problem. Their thinking is the problem. . . . Ultimately, however, conflict lies not in objective reality, but in people's heads. Truth is simply one more argument—perhaps a good one, perhaps not—for dealing with the difference. . . . Fears, even if ill founded, are real fears and need to be dealt with. Hopes, even if unrealistic, may cause war. Facts, even if established, do nothing to solve the problem. . . . As useful as looking for objective reality can be, it is ultimately the reality as each side sees it that constitutes the problem in a negotiation and opens the way to a solution.[7]

In negotiating your differences, be composed, thoughtful, and considerate of others. You achieve the best outcome for all concerned when you put your thinking cap on and address the issues that plague you. Remember, as perceptions will differ you need to listen carefully to what another is saying before you can negotiate an agreement.

Core Truth #17: No One Is Going to Agree with You All the Time, Unless Their Brain Is Turned Off

Need I say more? On the other hand, I'm reminded of Albert Einstein's sage words: "The definition of insanity is doing the same thing over and over again and expecting different results." Ludicrous as it seems, I think a lot of people turn off their brains by not wanting to know that there are many inventive ways to tackle conflicts.

Core Truth #18: When in Doubt, Don't Do Anything Until You Get More Viable Information

So much of the previous discussions in this book have had to do with the need to expand our perspective, see the big picture, accommodate another person's point of view, and so on. By staying open-minded and keeping your eyes and ears alert, you will acquire more knowledge and develop more empathy. Both can only help you when you sit down at the bargaining table to handle your conflicts.

I once attended a lecture that included, among other things, a discussion about "negative knowledge." The lecturer drew a large circle on the board and then did the following:

- He shaded a little slice of pie and labeled it "what we know."
- He shaded another little slice of pie next to the first and labeled this one "what we know we don't know."

- And finally, he labeled the enormous white space that remained inside the pie "what we don't know we don't know."

I found the size of that huge white space quite exciting.

When you are about to speak, about to make any kind of commitment, or about to make a major decision, stop and consider. Have you gathered all the information you need? Would any further details change what you are about to say, commit to, or decide? If you are stymied by a dispute and don't know what to do next, stop and reflect. What additional information could make a difference?

Think about the very best physician you know. Excellent doctors are always on the lookout for that one special symptom that could make the difference in a successful diagnosis. You may have had the experience of going to five qualified doctors who could not help you, only to go to a sixth doctor who noticed something critical that the first five did not. Approach your challenges with this kind of medical mind-set, and make it your lifelong quest to diminish the extent of your negative knowledge.

Core Truth #19: Assumptions Are like a Sieve—They Don't Hold Water

Assumptions are, by definition, made without conscious thought. We all make assumptions and we don't even know it. We just assume we are right, we know best, or our partner knows what we want.

One of the four agreements in Don Miguel Ruiz's book is:

Don't Make Assumptions: Find the courage to ask questions and to express what you really want. Communicate with others as clearly as you can to avoid misunderstandings, sadness and drama. With just this one agreement, you can completely transform your life.

Ruiz goes on to explain:

> The problem with making assumptions is that we *believe* they are the truth. We could swear they are real. We make assumptions about what others are doing or thinking. . . . Because we are afraid to ask for clarification, we make assumptions, and believe we are right about the assumptions; then we defend our assumptions and try to make someone else wrong. . . . Making assumptions in relationships leads to a lot of fights, a lot of difficulties, a lot of misunderstanding with people we supposedly love. . . . We also make assumptions about ourselves, and this creates a lot of inner conflict.[8]

Conflict is the product of individual differences, unrealistic expectations, insufficient information, inadequate communication, and, sometimes, malicious intent. It exposes your vulnerabilities, tests your courage, and challenges your assumptions. The opportunity is there for you to rethink your values, ponder your choices, take back your power, make amends for any transgressions, and hike up the high road with acts of kindness, caring, acceptance, and forgiveness.

Core Truth #20: For Every Action, Be It Verbal or Nonverbal, There Is a Consequence

People can forgive the occasional hurtful remark, lapse in communication, selfish slipup, or thoughtless act. Peace and harmony can be restored after a flare-up, provided there is an appropriate, heartfelt apology followed by a period of restorative calm. However, repeated transgressions—the arguments that don't get settled, the continuous mean-spirited complaints—are debilitating to relationships and have a toxic cumulative effect.

I first learned about a concept called the rain barrel when I was reading up on allergies. I found out that the human body is capable of handling numerous minor allergic assaults, but the effect is cumulative. For example, you may eat three strawberries and have no symptoms, but when you eat the fourth strawberry, you develop itchy hives. That fourth strawberry caused your "rain barrel" to overflow, and your body could no longer handle the cumulative allergic load.

I believe we all have a rain barrel for injustices as well. Some of my clients have a teacup, while others have a reservoir, but everyone has a limit. People may tolerate your occasional transgression, but if you continue to take advantage of their good nature, the rain barrel will fill to the brim, and they will hit their limit. At that point—if you reach it—expect there to be consequences for your behavior.

I had an enormous rain barrel when I was living with my first husband, who terrified me. He must have assumed I had unlimited tolerance, because for years I tolerated the situation. One day my rain barrel finally started to overflow, and that was the first day of the rest of my life.

Questions for Reflection

- Do you tend be pessimistic or optimistic?
- Are you a follower or a leader at home? At work?
- Do you prefer to tell others what to do or follow another's direction?
- Do you commonly make assumptions rather than ask questions of yourself and others?
- Are you the martyr who does too much and gets no rewards for your efforts?
- Do you sometimes feel like a victim because others let you down?
- Are you frequently overwhelmed by conflict and so exhausted you feel as if you are walking on empty?

Journaling

As you reflect on the preceding meaty questions, write about your energy level in regard to any of your conflicted relationships. Write about the people who drive you crazy and the times when they and you feel justifiably cross. Mention if accusations fly back and forth, because each person thinks, "I'm correct" or "I'm right," and, "You are mistaken" or "You are wrong." Then be honest with yourself and write about the consequences of your conduct when you feel like a victim.

If you are a quiet, soft-spoken Conflict Avoider, then write about how you relate to others when you offend them. In other words, what do you expect from them? When it's a matter of your integrity, write about whether you do or don't take responsibility for your actions. I commend you for digging deep into these particularly weighty matters.

8

How to Prevent Conflicts from Escalating

U sually arguments occur after we have been on the receiving end of too much sarcasm, blame, criticism, deceit, or malicious gossip. Sometimes arguments erupt because we have been nursing a grudge for days, weeks, or too many long years. Angry escalations quickly plunge our relationships into a maelstrom of divisiveness and despair.

The law of the jungle is not a sane way to settle your disputes. You are making matters worse than need be by turning your arguments into long-winded verbal brawls. It takes less than ten seconds to be screaming at the top of your lungs, your blood pressure rising, your heart thumping away. You are enraged because you had a bad day at the office, you were too busy to eat and now you are hungry, you stayed out late last night and you are too tired, or you have nothing else to do but pick a fight. In fact, it's not unusual to argue when you are lonely because this is how you get negative attention, which is better than none at all.

Arguments escalate when we are in the throes of hostile verbal attacks that seesaw back and forth, giving each person ample time to dump his or her emotional garbage on the other. For some of us, the shouting gets louder and louder, and that alone is enough to drive us crazy. Often people say hurtful things they don't really mean. Cutting remarks are impossible to take back, even if we immediately regret saying them. They certainly aren't worth the risk, because the injured person will never forget them. Unless the other person is exceptionally forgiving, he or she may be bitter indefinitely or even take the argument to the next level by seeking revenge—or by cutting off communication altogether.

I strongly encourage you to take precautions against ramping up your senseless arguments that are so distressing. Escalated disputes are not necessary in relationships.

Keeping Your Relationships Healthy

Friends do good deeds for one another. We encourage our loved ones and friends and share the good times with them. We pray when there is illness, trauma, or difficult conflicted relationships and give others more supportive attention because it is urgently needed. Satisfying marriages, strong family ties, and collegial friendships improve our health and longevity. As we encourage others, we benefit as much as they do. A network of warm, compassionate relations helps us stay alert and healthy. Close, meaningful friendships are a viable means of taking care of our body, mind, and soul. Multiple avenues are open for us to make trusting friendships that serve to inspire and enrich our lives.

Picture a magnificent, towering tree—so tall, so strong, and so beautiful, from its heaviest branches to its most delicate buds. Imagine its thick green foliage, a canopy of summer leaves rustling and protecting you from the hot sun. Maybe you are sitting at the base of this great tree, leaning your back against the trunk, taking a rest after a long walk. Like this tree, your friendships are rooted deep in trust yet reach as high as the heavens. They can support and protect you even as you appreciate and sustain them.

In his book *Social Intelligence*, Daniel Goleman explains that taking care of our relationships is actually an important way to take care of ourselves:

> The most striking finding on relationships and physical health is that socially integrated people—those who are married, have close family and friends, belong to social and religious groups, and participate widely in these networks—recover more quickly from disease and live longer. Roughly eighteen studies show a strong connection between social connectivity and mortality.[1]

Here's an idea: starting today, give your important relationships a little extra TLC (tender loving care). Offer plenty of encouragement (to refresh your memory, go back to step 7 in Chapter 6). Revitalize your relationships by laughing *with* others, not *at* them. We can't avoid our differences, but we don't have to magnify them so they appear greater than they already are. Remove the Mischief-Makers—blame, criticism, scorekeeping, competition, bias, deception, malicious gossip, meddling, vengefulness, amateur analysis, projection, and personalization—from your repertoire.

Following are guidelines for friendly behavior that will help you prevent a conflict from escalating:

- Take a deep breath, settle down, and show your tolerant nature.
- Acknowledge that you can't change control freaks, know-it-alls, or anyone else because that is up to them.
- Treat *everyone* with kindness and respect.
- Take an interest in others' interests.
- Never upbraid, criticize, blame, or chastise loved ones, friends, or coworkers.
- Set firm limits in regard to what conduct you will or will not tolerate.

- Be available, supportive, and encouraging when it is appropriate to do so.
- Recommit to your own integrity.

If you have broken someone's trust, you must confess your lies and be accountable and responsible for restoring the integrity that others expect from you. Implicit trust means you are loyal, reliable, and dependable and you consistently do what you say you will do. Trust is based on deeds performed, not promises forgotten. You can refresh your memory about being trustworthy by going to Chapter 6 and rereading the discussion about step 5, Be Honest, and Earn the Trust Others Place in You.

Psychotherapist John Amodeo reminds us that rebuilding trust is an ongoing process:

> Being honest with ourselves and others involves a lifelong process of growth. Since our self-knowledge is always limited, we can expect we will make mistakes. The important thing is to learn and grow from our errors of judgment. Failure provides the raw material for future success. Many of us who strive compulsively for perfection rarely take meaningful risks, because we believe if we're not successful, then a nagging inadequacy will be exposed.[2]

Take the occasional "meaningful risk" if it will benefit your relationships. You can't change other people, nor is it your job to do so. But you can change yourself. What qualities about yourself would you like to fix? Perhaps it will help you to keep an image in mind.

Being a Mensch

Mensch is a Yiddish word for a man who is decent, honorable, and responsible and who has strength of character. My mother often referred to a mensch as "a prince of a man." When I married Mark, I remember thinking that he was a prince of a man.

The mensch's motto is "Modesty is the best policy because we don't have to know it all." A mensch has fundamental decency and is someone worthy of respect. A mensch is an upstanding individual who:

Is humble
Is unselfish
Doesn't flaunt self-importance
Does good deeds
Takes responsibility for his actions
Doesn't exploit others
Is reliable and trustworthy
Has fortitude
Lives a life of integrity

In 2006 *New York Times* columnist Paul Krugman asked, "Where have all the mensches gone?" He wrote, "The people now running America aren't mensches." In fact, he referred to George W. Bush, Dick Cheney, and others as "anti-mensches."[3]

The famous Rabbi Abraham Joshua Heschel quotes Søren Kierkegaard's insightful message "Most people have no notion at all of the superiority by which a man transcends himself."[4] Rabbi Heschel gives us a remarkable message of hope:

The greatest sin of man is to forget that he is a prince—that he has royal power. All worlds are in need of exaltation, and everyone is charged to lift what is low, to unite what lies apart, to advance what is left behind. . . . And man is called upon to bring about the climax slowly but decisively. Nothing, therefore, is accidental. Even an intruding thought does not come at random. A thought is like a person. It arrives because it needs to be restored. A thought severed, abused, seeks to be reunited with its root. Furthermore, it may be a message to remind a man of a task, a task he was born to carry out.[5]

These memorable words inspire us to keep the faith and emulate those we know to be trustworthy, and then we learn to trust ourselves. Remember Core Truth #3, You Are the Center of Your World, but You Are Not the Center of the Universe. That opens the door whereby you utilize your power for the good of humankind, and therein is the potential for you to achieve inner peace.

Watch Your Voice and Smile

If you are having a conversation that runs the risk of escalating into an argument, I suggest speaking in a friendly, matter-of-fact tone—the same voice that you use when you are shopping for groceries or buying an automobile. This is just another conversation in your day. Use a pleasant, accepting tone. Speak gently and with respect. Your voice has the power to reassure and soothe the other person.

In her book *The Gentle Art of Verbal Self-Defense*, Suzette Elgin emphasizes the importance of voice quality as follows:

Voice "quality" is a mysterious thing. It involves pitch and nasality and volume and breathiness and harshness and timbre . . . but learning to control each one of them consciously and blend all those separate controls into a natural whole is probably impossible.

. . . If your voice is perceived by others as "whiny" . . . your utterances are going to be perceived that way, too—and your personality. If your voice is perceived as gruff and harsh and badly controlled, you are likely to be considered a bully;

if it is breathless and badly controlled, people will assume that you are slightly feather-headed and untrustworthy. . . . (It would not be an overstatement to say that getting rid of an unpleasant voice quality is even more important than any of the other techniques, since it can in fact invalidate all the rest of your skills.)[6]

I agree that poor voice quality can sabotage your other efforts at appearing calm, optimistic, kind, and deferential. If you are saying pleasant words but your voice is annoying, the other person is going to get annoyed.

It is common wisdom that if you smile before you pick up the telephone, the person on the other end will "hear" your smile. Smiling makes you appear confident and optimistic. Also, research has shown that just the process of deliberately moving the muscles of your face into a smile actually makes you feel better. (Beware: deliberately scowling makes you feel worse!) Remember to put on your happy face when you talk to others, not only to put them at ease but also to create optimistic feelings within yourself.

Keep Your Eyes on the Prize

People use sarcasm, cynicism, and disapproval when they believe they are better, smarter, or more deserving than someone else. I recommend that you leave these types of behaviors at the door and these types of judgments up to God. If you care about a relationship, let the other person bask in your approval and appreciation.

There is no concealing the venom that drips from our mouths when we are sarcastic. The surprising thing about sarcasm is that we don't always recognize it in our own voices. I remember the first time I actually heard myself lecturing my first husband, telling him how I thought he *should* change. Well, I got a real eye-opener when I heard my veiled anger. I truly didn't know that I was being sarcastic, even though it was quite evident that I disapproved of his behavior. Then it occurred to me that I unwittingly might be upsetting others in my life with my cynical attitude and sarcastic tone.

We quickly take offense when we hear cutting remarks directed at us, but we turn a deaf ear to our own snide way of speaking to others. We let others know that we disapprove of them by our patronizing voice and attitude of contempt. Then, not so surprisingly, others attack us back.

When Carrie and Frank came to my office, I could see immediately that they were accustomed to sniping at each other. Frank treated Carrie as if her choices about where to sit and what to say were all stupid. Carrie regarded Frank like some kind of imbecile who was unqualified to give advice. Yet all they both wanted from each other was approval.

Carrie said, "I feel so worthless when Frank is condescending to me."

Frank said, "Carrie doesn't even have to say anything; she just rolls her eyes."

Carrie said, "Frank is so sarcastic, he drives me crazy."

Frank said, "Carrie scowls at me and I get a knot in my stomach."

I said, "Carrie and Frank, without realizing it, both of you are acting like Conflict Antagonists. You are defensive and hypersensitive to criticism yet disapproving of each other at the same time. In other words, you can dish it out, but you can't take it. You wanted a perfect union, but instead you have almost destroyed your relationship because you are not having any fun. Do you realize how much you are torturing each other with your snide remarks? And do you realize how difficult it is to have a loving relationship when you are both feeling defensive? How do you expect to settle your differences when you treat each other with contempt so much of the time? Do you hear the sarcasm in your voices?"

Frank said, "I know I get cynical at times. My mother gets moody, and she's sarcastic when she talks to my sister and me."

Carrie said, "I can tell by Frank's voice that he's being arrogant and mean."

I handed the partners paper and pen and told them to circle the words in the following list that fit their image of a healthy relationship:

Love
Disrespect
Disapproval
Support
Respect
Kindness
Revenge
Approval
Encouragement
Retaliation

Carrie and Frank laughed because they had circled the same words: love, respect, support, kindness, encouragement, and approval.

This exercise was not meant to be an IQ test. It was simply meant to show in a concrete manner that they both valued the same things. They had learned through this simple exercise what the prize was. Now they had to learn how to keep their eyes on it!

Next I said, "I want you to look directly at each other and repeat after me: 'Damn it, I'm not perfect and I never will be!'"

The first time, Frank and Carrie were hesitant. They thought perhaps I had lost my mind. Then I asked the couple to repeat this sentence three more times. By the final repetition, they were shouting.

Carrie laughed and said, "I'm going to use this as my mantra!"

I said, "Now, there are two parts to your homework. First, I am suggesting that you monitor your critical, contemptuous thoughts. Every time you recognize your negative thinking, substitute a positive thought. You might have to shift gears five or twenty-five times a day; just do your best.

"Second, I want you to listen to your sarcastic voice and compare that to your cordial voice. It's also a good idea to make a habit of monitoring your facial expressions so you aren't scowling at each other, because when you smile that means you are friendly instead of frightening each other."

I met with Frank and Carrie two weeks later and asked them how their homework was working out.

Frank said, "Being optimistic is taking a huge weight off my shoulders! Carrie and I are nicer to each other, and lately I have had more time and energy to finish some projects I'd put off doing. We really aren't fighting anymore."

Carrie said, "I'm concentrating on being kind to Frank. I can't believe how liberating this is. Now that I'm respectful to Frank, he's more loving to me."

By putting the health of their relationship first and keeping their eyes on the prize, Frank and Carrie were able to set aside their mean-spirited remarks. In turn, their mutual kindness made their lives more pleasant, which made them feel more cheerful and less critical. What goes around comes around.

Accusations and Allegations: True or False?

Accusations are about nitpicking for flaws. When you clash and fight, accusations do considerable harm to your close relationships.

Accusations are finger-pointing attacks: censure, blame, criticism, faultfinding, and complaints. The allegations could be true, partially true, or utterly untrue.

If someone is picking on you, remember that their accusations are based on their view of reality. Accusations are always about your worst behavior and don't take into account what you are doing that is right and positive.

Without thinking, Conflict Antagonists automatically defend themselves against their accuser and get downright nasty. Suddenly they are battling it out as insults mount and their interactions get ugly. Responding in kind is the fastest way to escalate conflict. Conflict Avoiders are likely to be intimidated. Conflict Fixers may get their feelings hurt. Conflict Goof-Ups may feel ashamed and/or aggressive. Conflict Innovators, however, make a concerted effort not to be defensive. They keep an open mind and are willing to see a kernel of truth in others' accusations. They can even admit their flaws to their accuser, which robs accusations of their destructive power.

The Clothespin Strategy

The clothespin strategy is a special physical and mental energy saver that instantly prevents you from opening your mouth so you won't be tempted to say anything you will later regret. Anytime you encounter a caustic person and you are tempted to retort with a scathing remark, the clothespin strategy works wonders.

Rather than further sabotage your conflicted relationships, take a huge imaginary clothespin and place it on your mouth. I tell my clients to pretend that their clothespin is painted a bright color—mine is bright yellow. You can decorate your clothespin or keep it plain. My imaginary yellow clothespin has prevented me from saying many inappropriate remarks that would have damaged my relationships and been embarrassing to recollect later.

The clothespin strategy teaches you self-control. My client Cynthia said, "The clothespin strategy is great! I keep an actual clothespin in the kitchen, one in the bedroom, and one in my

192 I Hate Conflict!

purse." With that she opened her handbag and pulled out a tiny, plain wooden clothespin, and we both started to laugh. Cynthia said, "You have to tell people about this strategy because it really works well for me!"

The clothespin strategy is a prudent way to stop any bickering, blaming, criticizing, or malicious gossiping. Use this strategy anytime you are feeling upset and are ready to blab or to tell somebody off.

How to Defuse a Tense Situation

Even though I was preaching the hazards of blame and criticism to all my clients, my husband Mark and I would occasionally play the blame game. We decided to come up with a strategy that would keep us from falling into the blaming trap.

This is how it works: whenever we had the urge to blame, we agreed to say something silly. Mark and I decided to say, "Who should we blame, Clinton or global warming?" during the years that Bill Clinton was our president. Every time we said these words, we would laugh—partly because it was funny and partly because we were so relieved to have headed off a totally unnecessary argument. For a bonus, we got a big bear hug and a kiss. By that time, whatever had been bugging us was a nonissue and our blaming or criticizing was totally meaningless.

If you have gotten into the habit of blaming your partner, I suggest you agree on a word or phrase that will make you both stop in your tracks. Use whatever you want. "Train wreck." "Holy cow!" "Slippery sideways." "Beggars and thieves." No one will know the meaning of this phrase except you, which is part of the fun. When you make a habit of laughing instead of blaming, you reap the rewards of being friends once again.

Apologizing

From time to time in this book, I have recommended making a heartfelt apology as a way to get a relationship back on track. If you have done or said something of which you are not proud, you need to offer a genuine apology, as well as continue to invest your energies in strengthening your relationship. In so doing, you will have less guilt and remorse.

Rather than escalate your arguments, humbly apologize for any mistake, misjudgment, misunderstanding, or memory lapse. Express your regret for any unkind remark or audacious assumption. A sincere apology is meaningful when you speak from your heart, showing you care. Then you are authentic; then you are earnest; then you are genuine and kind. In turn, you reap the rewards of a dignified discussion with no finger-pointing, fault-finding aggravation.

Remember that when you crossed the line, you lost your credibility and integrity. The other person has no reason to continue talking to you because you demonstrated you are willing to do mortal damage to your relationship. By making your apology genuine, you make vital inroads in repairing your conflicted relationship.

Be frank, responsible, and trustworthy. Your facial expressions and demeanor will to a large extent indicate whether you truly are repentant or not. The following are honest statements that mean you take your apology seriously:

- "I apologize for being nasty and hurting your feelings."
- "I've been a cad; I'm sorry I lied to you."
- "I apologize for being rude to you."
- "I apologize for ignoring what you told me."
- "I'm sorry I've been a Scrooge. I won't be so stingy the next time."

- "I've been a poor sport, and I apologize for not thinking about what matters to you the most."
- "I'm sorry. I wasn't in my right mind, and I apologize for abandoning you."

The best apology is specific about what you did wrong and indicates how you will compensate the other person for your bad behavior. You must be empathetic and acknowledge how you have hurt or offended another. You must briefly explain what you have learned from this unfortunate experience. When you mention how you will change your conduct, then you set the stage for restoring your trusting relationship, step by step.

When children grow up in a family in which they have never heard an apology from their parents or caregivers, the very idea of saying, "I'm sorry; I apologize for my bad behavior," seems strange or absurd. If you are in any doubt about whether or not an apology is called for, go ahead and apologize. If by chance your apology was not necessary, the other person will still be happy to hear that you care enough about your relationship to make sure everything is going well.

There will always be some people who refuse to apologize for their inappropriate behavior. Their motto is, "I never apologize to anyone. I never have and I never will." You can request an apology from these people, nag or shame them into apologizing, or just be mad at them for not apologizing. If the other person does not believe there is a need to apologize, you and I know this is a blatant lie, because no one is perfect all of the time. And if you want to tell the liar what I have said, be my guest and do so—and then tell me what happened next.

A word of caution: some folks apologize and then turn around and make the same foolish errors again and again. A habitual apology is useless.

My client Rachael told me a work-related story that involved a remarkable apology. "I was in the middle of a sales meeting,"

Rachael said, "when my manager suddenly got really mad at one of the guys and shouted at him, 'You are *stupid* and you *do not* know what you are doing!' Then he stormed out of the room and slammed his office door shut. There were eight of us in the room, all dumbfounded, wondering what was going on. In about five minutes, our manager returned to the conference room, sat back down in his chair, and simply said, 'I apologize; I was acting like a baby.'" Rachael told me, "Now there is one enlightened soul!"

Calming Meditation

Instead of being agitated and upset, I recommend you take five to ten minutes to reap the reward of a calming meditation. It's easy.

1. Relax by closing your eyes and paying attention to your breathing.
2. Notice if your heartbeat is rapid or slow.
3. Keep your mouth closed, and inhale a deep belly breath.
4. Then very slowly exhale through your open mouth.
5. Repeat breathing this way for one minute.

You might note that your heartbeat is already slowing down. Do this meditation for one minute and enjoy the soothing effect.

To deepen your meditation, keep your eyes closed and breathe normally in and out. Then focus on one area of your body that is telling you, "I'm stressed out—pay attention to me." Do this for one minute. If another area of your body needs attention, then put your focus on that spot. This is simple—no thinking required.

Now you are ready for a much deeper meditation. My favorite is "Opening the Energy Centers." I have extrapolated upon this meditation from Shakti Gawain and refer to it as the "Golden Light." Imagine that a brilliant golden light is shining above your head. Then pretend that golden strands of light are swirling around inside of your head. Feel the warmth of sunlight on your face and neck. Then let the golden light fill your torso, arms, back, chest, and abdomen and into your thighs, calves, ankles, and toes. Bask in the golden strands that move about in your body. Enjoy the golden light and the warm sensations you feel.

Now notice that the golden strands of light are moving over your head and down the right side of your body, past your neck and arms, down around the bottom of your feet, and then up the left side of your body. Wrap the golden strands of light up over your head and down your body like this three times. Then reverse the direction of the golden strands of light and bring them down the left side of your body and back up the right side. Do this three times. When you are finished, allow the golden glow to stay with you a little longer, if you have the time. Slowly open your eyes and let the afterglow stay with you as long as possible. Gawain states, "When you finish this meditation, you will be deeply relaxed yet energized and exhilarated."[7]

These simple ways of meditating are refreshing enough to potentially ease your stress so you can sustain a calm demeanor. The benefits of meditation are amazing. Your mood will lift. You might be inspired to make significant changes in your attitude. You might even be encouraged to make friends with your enemies.

Questions for Reflection

Take two minutes to reflect on the following questions:

- Do you often start an argument?
- Do you argue because someone else starts the argument?
- In the scheme of things, are your arguments about vital issues?
- Did you contact a close friend so you could vent your anger instead of arguing?
- Did you consult with a counselor, a coach, a mediator, a minister, or anyone else who would give you a different slant on the ravages of arguing?

Journaling

As you answer the crucial questions for reflection, you will have much to ponder. Write about your experiences growing up, and think about the times when you clashed with your parents, siblings, or friends. Describe in your journal how you justify telling another person off. Consider what it would be like if you were scrupulously honest with yourself, and write about any tendencies you might have to be in denial because you tell yourself half-truths. As you humbly look inward, describe the ways you get defensive and make excuses for your conduct. If you never heard your parents apologize for their wrongdoings, write about how this grabs you right now. If you have not apologized for a time when your conduct was inappropriate, write about whether you believed you had good reasons for not saying, "I regret how I treated you." And if you thought the other person should apologize first, write down your rationale on this testy topic. Now if you are the one to express regret first, describe how this makes you feel toward others. Take your time in thinking and writing about these weighty issues—you are likely to learn some healthy relationship insights. Next, write about the healthy ways that you unwind or calm down and keep conflict from escalating.

9

Confront with Confidence

I'll never forget my first bona fide confrontation. My first husband and I had opened a small retail shoe store, and Noreen was our first employee. She was nineteen years old and a well-mannered, competent salesperson, but she had one noticeable flaw: a strong body odor. I knew we had to do something about this, but it was an awkward predicament. I thought my husband should take care of it, but much to my chagrin, he dumped the confrontation on me when he shouted, "I'm not doing any such thing—you do it!" I thought what a coward he was. It was incongruous to me that this man could be an abrasive Conflict Antagonist inflicting his rage on our three children and me, but he was too wimpy to confront Noreen. And how could it be that I, the meek-little-mouse-wife, too terrified to confront my own husband, would have to manage this conflict?

I didn't protest, because I knew my husband wasn't going to budge. Now I had to figure out how I was going to approach Noreen, because I had never before been put in such a discomfited situation. For sure, I knew I would trip over my tongue if I didn't have a plan.

The next day, I trembled as I looked directly at Noreen and said, "This is awkward for me to say, but I don't think you are aware that you have a body odor."

Noreen looked aghast. Somehow this problem had escaped her notice. I nodded and took a container of deodorant from my purse and handed it to her saying, "Noreen, I use this brand. Try it and see how it works for you."

Noreen blushed and said, "I appreciate your telling me, and thank you for the deodorant; that is a big help." The dreaded deed was done, and I settled down.

I have learned much about confrontation from my experience with Noreen and my clients. Basically, confrontations must be planned in advance in order for them to be successful. Keep in mind that the challenge of confrontation is to state your dissatisfaction with another and set limits on the conduct that you will or will not tolerate.

You might feel as if you are on shaky ground. Necessary confrontations occur for good reasons. You confront for your health's sake, to save your sanity, to mend broken fences, and to restore trust.

Must I Confront?

My client Julie asked, "Is it best to confront someone when they tick me off, or should I say nothing and dismiss it?"

The following are key questions to ask yourself:

- What is the purpose of your confrontation?
- What do you hope to gain by confronting?
- How do you anticipate others will respond if you politely confront them?
- In the event you do have a confrontation, what outcome are you seeking?

The biggest mistake you can make is to intuitively know in your gut that you should confront someone yet not be willing to do it. Some common fears of confrontation are:

- The outcome seems too uncertain.
- You are afraid you will handle the discussion the wrong way.
- You worry that others will not behave in a reasonable manner.
- You are too ashamed or distraught to begin.
- You fear being overpowered or rejected.
- You aren't prepared.
- You are scared a confrontation might jeopardize your close connection.
- You don't want to be misinterpreted.
- You loathe the thought that confrontation might lead to more arguments.

Under certain circumstances, confronting someone is not advisable, even if your cause is just. Do *not* attempt confrontation if any of the following apply:

- You do not feel safe because the other individual is unreasonable.
- You fear the other person could assault you (violence and/or sexual abuse).
- The other person is intoxicated, under the influence of illegal drugs, or overdosing on prescription medication.
- Either you or the other person is ill or incapacitated for any reason.
- The timing is inappropriate because other priorities (such as getting kids off to school, dashing off to an important meeting, or making an urgent phone call) take precedence.

Foremost, know that getting to the core of any convincing confrontation requires diplomacy and prudent judgment. A well-thought-out confrontation enables you to accomplish what you initially thought would be a torturous ordeal.

Think About What You Want to Accomplish

You are ready to begin your confrontation when you are certain you will argue no more. You will address the problem, negotiate a solution, and put it behind you.

Think about a conflicted area in your life that you know you need to address. Imagine it as a huge wave coming right at you. It's so close you can see sunlight through the turquoise wall of water, and you notice the top of the wave is starting to crest and turn white. Take a deep breath . . . and get on your surfboard! This is the best possible wave for you, and you are about to catch it at the best possible time and have the ride of your life. You are on a path that will establish your credibility, reliability, and responsibility.

Your goal in resolving your difficulties is *not* to "win" or to be able to say, "I told you so." You do *not* want to hurt or blame others. You *do* want to do the following:

- Spare others the embarrassment of being wrong.
- Do what is in the best interests of each party.
- Be tactful and approach your disputes in a dignified manner.
- Resolve the issue once and for all.

Determined Conflict Innovators do not let contentious issues pile up. They take the bull by the horns and address their conflicts, one at a time. They take a deep breath and go straight to the core issues. Because they have thought about it, they know in advance that they will either compromise, wait and see, or agree to disagree.

How Much Are You Willing to Compromise?

In our conflicted world, nobody gets everything they want. When I think of positive trade-offs, I think of bargaining. I ask my clients what they are willing to give up to get a desired outcome from others. Think of bargaining in the marketplace, in politics, and in government. The same process of negotiating applies to your conflicts. Making nonverbal agreements, verbal agreements, and written agreements are beneficial for all concerned in any arena where controversy prevails.

Before you have your confrontation, think about any compromises or concessions you might be willing to make. If you are not willing to give one inch, then you have a nonnegotiable issue (see the next section). In general, the more patient, accepting, and forgiving you are, the easier it is to reach an agreement. You do not need to relent your position altogether, but if you are willing to negotiate, you might find out that there are viable alternative options to consider. When you agree, you are cooperatively working as a team, and this helps you discover a practical compromise.

Nonnegotiable Issues: Agreeing to Disagree

There is no point in arguing or trying to convince others to agree with you when they have made up their mind and nothing is going to dissuade them. In that case, it is wise to be accommodating and accept their position. I've learned that whether nonnegotiable issues are insignificant or weighty, the energy people expend in defending them is much the same.

My work with couples indicates that approximately one-third of all conflicted issues are nonnegotiable. There are topics about which couple communication persistently proves to be unproductive. Neither partner will change his or her mind about the issue, whether it is spoiling the kids, which football team to cheer for, or the need to buy a holiday present for Aunt Jean. The best couples can do is agree to disagree and never discuss the matter again.

My client Mandy is a die-hard Democrat, and her husband, Chuck, is a dyed-in-the-wool Republican. Mandy told me, "Chuck and I could not talk about politics without becoming frantic with each other. We did not agree with one another, and there was nothing either of us could say that would be constructive. When we tried to express our differing opinions, we would go round and round and it was exhausting. I knew Chuck was not about to change his political views and neither was I."

Chuck said, "I saw no point in arguing about politics. Some people like to quarrel, but I don't. Mandy and I had a frank discussion, and we made an agreement that we wouldn't talk about politics."

Mandy replied, "Thank goodness we've been able to keep our promise, and now our relationship is better than ever. Sometimes I have to bite my tongue, but saving the aggravation is worth it."

I was talking to my client Terry, who told me his sensitive predicament. He said, "Martha was out of town when I happened to bump into Sharon, an old friend of ours. Sharon asked me to have lunch with her, and I thought that would be nice. I had some time to kill before my board meeting. It was all so innocent. Later that evening I told Martha that I had had lunch with Sharon. She was incensed! For the next couple of hours, I tried to explain to Martha that everything was on the up-and-up. After all, we've both been friends with Sharon for many long years. I never dreamt Martha would react that way. I didn't see anything wrong with what I did, but Martha was extremely upset. Now she has made it quite clear that I'm never to have lunch or dinner with another woman unless she is present. I love Martha, so I will honor her wishes, even though I don't agree with her."

If it's all the same to you, then yield in the spirit of giving without expecting to receive in return. At a later date, the other person might be more willing to accommodate a request of yours. If you really are not happy about conceding, my coaching experience indicates that long-held perspectives and cherished opinions can often be negotiated, mediated, and successfully managed. Even if you must give in to an ultimatum, you may be able to get the other person to soften his or her position or agree to some concessions that you would find helpful.

Nonnegotiable Issues: When It's Your Way or the Highway

Sometimes you will be the one who has a nonnegotiable issue. You may feel so strongly about the need for your teenager to avoid drugs, the need for your partner to stop drinking, or the need for your aged father to stop driving that you are not interested in talking about a watered-down semicommitment on the issue. A confrontation about a nonnegotiable issue is more about presentation than give-and-take. The other person must be willing to surrender, because your demand must prevail.

When nonnegotiable issues such as this come up, it means certain behavior seriously upsets you or offends your code of honor. Let's be clear about these situations—the stakes are very high, and compromise is not acceptable. These issues are important enough to make or break your loving connections with others in your life. Assuming you do not want a falling-out or angry confrontation, you want to be as pleasant and as reasonable as possible presenting your case.

Nonnegotiable issues signal you to be alert and envision a yellow caution sign. Conflict Innovators tread lightly, knowing that they might get emotional about their controversial issue. If discussing your nonnegotiable issue starts to feel like a tug-of-war, with both sides thinking, "I'm right and you're wrong," then neither side is ready to talk. You cannot approach nonnegotiable matters when you are both invested in stubbornly trying to overpower one another. At the same time, something must be done, for if you do not end your standoff, a close family member or friend might drift away, or you might stay stuck indefinitely.

Lydia, a mother and grandmother, was worried about her brother, Allen. She said, "I'm fourteen years younger than Allen. He's pushing seventy, and there's a lot of dementia on our side of the family. Allen is in denial about his potential health issues as he ages. We talked about his getting long-term health-care insurance, but Allen didn't see any point in spending the money. I was losing sleep over this, because I plan to be his caregiver if he develops Alzheimer's disease. I kept thinking about what would happen if he became incapacitated. I couldn't put this issue out of my mind.

"Finally, one day I woke up and said, 'Allen, this issue is nonnegotiable. You must get long-term health-care insurance right away to ease my mind.' Even though Allen disagreed with me, I got the insurance policy and he signed it, saying, 'If it means that much to you, I'll do it.' It is such a relief to me that he has this extra financial protection. This gives me much more peace of mind."

Another client, Meg, talked to me at length about her boyfriend's drinking. The couple had discussed marriage, but Meg was afraid of marrying an alcoholic, as her mother had done. Eventually, Meg confronted Eddie and said, "If you don't get treatment for your alcoholism, I'm not going to marry you." Eddie replied, "I love you, Meg, and I want to marry you. If that's what it takes, I'll join an AA group. You are far more important to me than alcohol ever could be."

When you need to confront someone about a nonnegotiable issue, stay calm and put your commonsense thinking cap on. Keep it simple. Experience has taught me that men in particular have a limited attention span for such testy matters. They will listen to one-liners but will turn off their hearing when there is a lot of rambling going on. I recommend using the following opening statement: "I have a nonnegotiable issue that we need to address." Then get right to the point.

As you continue your confrontation, be friendly but firm. Avoid antagonism, and think "we," not "me."

If the other person cannot agree without gaining something in return, consider making some concessions in other areas. For example, let's say you tell your partner that she must stop abusing prescription medications. She says fine—provided you never reveal to anyone that she had this problem. You've got yourself a deal.

Another useful approach is reciprocity—or, put more simply, taking turns. Reciprocity is the fairest way to compromise without getting bogged down in senseless arguing: "You concede this time, and next time it's my turn to give in." There is always the chance that your conflicted relations will strengthen when you make reciprocal agreements.

When you are finished, shake hands and be proud that you have amicably achieved closure on this difficult subject. It's usually a relief when nonnegotiable issues are settled, even if we don't get our way.

When nonnegotiable issues are deadlocked, it's time to back off and regroup. Perhaps you need to cool down and rethink the direction you are taking. Perhaps there are concessions you can make so the other person might be inclined to bend to your nonnegotiable demand. In the event that negotiations break down and neither party trusts the other, then counseling, coaching, or mediation is highly recommended.

My husband Mark had an annoying habit of turning on all the house lights and leaving them on. In the great scheme of life, this is an inane issue, but it bothered me a lot. I must confess that our conflict spiraled out of control because I kept complaining and nagging whenever he neglected to turn the lights off—which was all the time. Then I would run around the house at bedtime and do the task myself.

Mark would repeatedly say that the cost of electricity was only a few pennies, implying that I was making a big deal over a trivial matter. I didn't see it Mark's way. I told him I thought we were spending money foolishly. Each time I mentioned turning off the lights, he discounted my point of view, and I got more indignant.

This very same conversation went on for ten years or more. It was such a ridiculous disagreement that it was scarcely worth discussing, but after ten years, it was wearing on my nerves. I knew Mark appreciated my frugal nature, but in this case he dismissed the fact that turning off the lights was important to *me* even if it was not important to *him*.

Then one auspicious day Mark shifted gears and stated in his most authoritative voice, "Lee, I want you to know that every day it is my job to *turn on* the lights, and every day it is your job to *turn off* the lights." I was literally speechless! I didn't know whether to laugh or cry.

Mark had made it plain to me how he meant to settle our harebrained dispute. I had the choice of continuing to try to get him to do it, which would mean more years of fruitless nagging, or accepting Mark's position. So in a flash, I thought it best to drop the matter.

Henceforth, every day Mark turned all the lights on, and every evening I made a point of turning the lights off because that was my job! Silly as it sounds, I learned an important lesson about how nonnegotiable issues can deeply affect our closest relations. Whenever I think of how absurd our differences of opinions were, I can't help but laugh, and that feels so good.

Plan Your Confrontation

A well-planned confrontation enables you to accomplish what you have shied away from for weeks, months, or years. For a long time you thought it was easier to capitulate and say nothing, but now you realize that the time has come to do some damage control.

A well-planned confrontation gives two or more people the opportunity to be candid and get their controversial issues on the table without being defensive, perhaps for the first time. Confrontations are not meant to be long-winded monologues about everything that has ever bothered you for many long years. Confrontations also are not meant to be devious, tricky, or unjust.

When you plan a confrontation, you have a deep conviction regarding the truth of your point of view. Many people mistake assertion for aggression. You need to be assertive, but you do not need to be aggressive. Make certain you are courteous and forthright and that you speak your truth. If you are aggressive, domineering, and ruthless, your aggressive stance will be construed as belligerence. Then in a blink, you will become just another boor.

There are many techniques that will help you keep a rational demeanor and be more at ease. Reread the seven steps and refresh your mind about the optimal behavior for confrontations and the phrases you can use.

1. Speak politely; common courtesies count.
2. Swallow your pride, and admit your mistakes.
3. Seek to understand; you have nothing to defend.
4. Show compassion, and keep the welfare of others in mind.
5. Be honest, and earn the trust others place in you.
6. Never wave a red flag at a raging bully.
7. Use encouragement and laughter to keep conflict at bay.

Because the key to confronting with confidence is preparation, here is a checklist:

- Choose your statements carefully. Think about, perhaps even practice out loud, what you are going to say.
- Talk to a close friend who can give you a lot of support and encouragement.
- Focus not on winning but on being constructive and making reasonable agreements.
- Decide if you want to be friends or foes.
- Try to imagine what this issue looks like from the other side. Inevitably, your perception of any given disagreement rarely will jive with the other person's point of view.
- Think about possible concessions you might make.
- Remind yourself over and over again that negativity breeds disappointment and failure, while optimism leads to success. In order to accomplish your goals in any arena of your life, focus on your hopeful thoughts and nurturing ideas, and throw out all the negative thoughts that creep into your mind.
- Be fearless. Never discount your own worth by putting yourself down.

A successful conversation has a fairly predictable path. Envision how you would like your discussion to go:

1. Both sides listen carefully at the outset as you present your issue.
2. Both sides present, honestly and in detail, what they want.
3. Both sides negotiate to reach the best outcome.
4. Trade-offs and concessions are made, and the haggling is concluded.
5. Signed agreements and a handshake confirm the deal is done!

With tongue in cheek, I tell my clients, "Up until today, you were in conflict preschool. Now you took a flying leap into conflict graduate school, and you are maturing and learning how to negotiate your differences in a dignified manner."

Think About Your Conflict Style— and Theirs

Edna said, "This is idiotic! I don't have trouble speaking up at work. I'm smart; they pay me a lot of money to supervise the nurses. But when it comes to telling my mother how I feel, I'm too scared to negotiate with her. She can be difficult, and that's why I'm stuck."

I said, "Edna, I believe your mother is a Conflict Goof-Up. From what you have told me, she is likely to say things that aren't true, to confuse the issues, and to deflect the conversation by making up something to put the blame on you. But if you are prepared for this kind of behavior, it won't throw you off as much."

Edna and I did some role-playing in my office for fun; I acted the part of her mother. I behaved like the most irresponsible, exasperating Conflict Goof-Up in the world. I threw in some nasty insults (with apologies to Edna) and generally tried to get Edna off topic.

Prepared for the worst, Edna confronted her mother. The conversation actually went much better than our role-playing!

Whatever your personal conflict style happens to be, this is the time to practice being a Conflict Innovator.

If you will be confronting a Conflict Avoider, remember that this person is as horrified by the conversation as you are. Conflict Avoiders are too intimidated to confront anyone. The very thought of it sets their nerves on edge, and their mind gets discombobulated with all kinds of extraneous stuff, so they change the subject or walk away, and nothing is said. Usually, Conflict Avoiders deny the wisdom of confronting because they have no experience in being assertive.

If you are a Conflict Avoider—and given that you picked up this book, that is more than likely—be brave. Stay focused. Remember, this confrontation is an opportunity to improve your life.

If you will be confronting a Conflict Fixer, be prepared for this person to interrupt with all kinds of bright ideas that are not actually helpful. Conflict Fixers are biased and unfair because they are so sure they know it all. Conflict Fixers want to settle their disputes yesterday. They get so antsy that they overstate their case and deliver a lecture.

If you are a Conflict Fixer, try to hold your tongue. Give a brief, reasonable explanation about the issue and the outcome you desire.

If you will be confronting a Conflict Goof-Up, get ready for chaos. Conflict Goof-Ups make a big fuss and panic because they don't know how to safely confront. They are likely to be confusing, insulting, and devious.

If you are a Conflict Goof-Up, this is your chance to prove you have turned over a new leaf. Show that you can think clearly and take responsibility for your behavior. If, in the past, you antagonized the person you are about to confront, it wouldn't hurt to apologize at the outset of your discussion.

If you will be confronting a Conflict Antagonist, be prepared for angry retorts and criticism. Conflict Antagonists act like a bull in a china shop when they attempt to confront. They are hopping mad and interested only in getting what they want. Arrogant Conflict Antagonists take a competitive stance that is much too heavy-handed. They aren't ready to negotiate or compromise because they are focused on "me," not "we," and they seem to have little or no concern for the value of their close connection.

If you are a Conflict Antagonist, rein in your hot temper, and keep in mind the importance of your relationship with the person you are going to confront. You goal is not to teach this person a lesson but to arrive at a mutually satisfactory compromise.

If you will be confronting a Conflict Innovator, it's your lucky day. Conflict Innovators are willing to make sacrifices for the good of their conflicted relationships. By treating others as friends, not foes, they acknowledge other points of view. They take an optimistic, hopeful attitude because that affects the outcome of their negotiations. Conflict Innovators speak respectfully, ask for information, try to clarify misunderstandings, and state clearly the limits of their tolerance for other people's inappropriate conduct.

If you are a Conflict Innovator, you are already a wise negotiator! You know how to discuss your differences politely and judiciously, how to keep your wits about you, and how to speak calmly and frankly. Conflict Innovators know they must focus on "we," not "me," in order to resolve differences with integrity.

In *Getting to Yes*, the authors give us a realistic perspective on the importance of focusing on "we," not "me":

> In any negotiation it is highly desirable to be sensitive to the values, perceptions, concerns, norms of behavior and mood of those with whom you are dealing. . . . The more successfully you can get in step with that person's way of thinking, the more likely you are to work out an agreement.[1]

Your ability to keep an open mind will, in all likelihood, make the difference between success and failure. Forget the issue of who is right and who is wrong. Be cheerful, optimistic, and open to the possibility of compromise.

Be Aware of Your Triggers

Common sense advises that you be aware of your hot buttons, so purposefully control your temper, no matter what the other person says or does. The seven steps enable you to make headway without losing control. You accomplish a formidable task when you calmly take charge, stand your ground, and say what needs to be said. Then you are ready to resolve your differences with anyone in your life.

Choosing the Time and Place

First, suggest a time and place to meet. That will give you time to get your bearings.

- "Let's have this conversation when we are both relaxed. How about Friday morning?"
- "I'm too unsettled to think clearly right now, but I would like to speak to you on Tuesday."
- "I'm sure we can work it out, so let's arrange a time to do that."

Choose a time and place where there will be no interruptions, and schedule enough time for a thorough discussion. Pick a day and time when you will not be hungry, sleepy, rushed, or distracted.

Getting Started

On the day of your confrontation:

- Get enough rest, so you are alert.
- Make sure you eat something, so you will be able to concentrate.
- Wear clothes in which you feel confident.
- Do not wear sunglasses indoors—they interfere with eye contact and make you look like you are hiding something.

- Relax as much as you can.
- Sit back in your chair. Don't lean forward, as this looks aggressive.
- Let your arms rest in your lap. Don't fold them across your chest, as this looks defensive.
- Put on your friendly face. Pay attention to your facial expression, and note the other person's demeanor. Do not scowl or giggle.
- Speak slowly and firmly as you would to the Queen of England.
- Be sure your attitude is hopeful and gracious.
- Stay in charge of your emotions at all times.
- Cry if you must, but no hysterical drama is allowed.

Remember to stay cool, be patient, keep your sense of humor handy, and show you care.

Before You Confront, Give Yourself a Pep Talk

Anytime you are too scared to attempt a confrontation, repeat the following sentences out loud three times a day for one week, and see if these encouraging words build your self-confidence:

"I will assert myself."
"I am important and expect to be treated with respect."
"I will confront, and then I won't let myself down."

Here are some more peppy reminders that might have you laughing aloud. Use these statements three times a day for a week, a month, or a year—as much time as you need to convince yourself that you can learn how to confront.

- "I am not a pushover."
- "I refuse to be henpecked."
- "I want to get the recognition I deserve."
- "I am not an easy target."
- "I am not a doormat."

Encourage yourself daily with reminders about all your excellent accomplishments. Take credit for past confrontations you handled successfully. In certain ways, you are already practiced and disciplined. You can do it again and achieve your goals! Think positive, and remember that when you learn how to calmly confront, it is far better than saying nothing.

Set Ground Rules

It is important to set some guidelines:

• **Schedule enough time.** This confrontation means a lot to you and everyone involved, so it is imperative that everyone agrees to spend as much time as it takes to reach a fair settlement. It's possible that, even though you made an appointment, the other person will be in a hurry. If he or she says, "I have fifteen minutes to get this done," this is not OK. It is disrespectful to you. Do not get intimidated and try to rush through your discussion. Instead, immediately offer to reschedule for another time when the other person does not have such pressing time constraints. If he or she insists that fifteen minutes should be enough, then you say, "Indeed, we should be able to wrap up our conversation quickly, but it is not fair to you to have this discussion when you clearly have so much on your mind." Of course, what you really mean is, do not trifle with me, this is important!

• **Long-winded complaints are not allowed.** Promise that you will cut to the chase, and ask others to be brief as well.

• **Make sure there will be no interruptions.** Keep your environment free of distractions and excessive noise. Turn off any cell phones, radios, televisions, and so on.

• **Alcohol and illegal drugs are not allowed.** If the other person shows up drunk, you are under no obligation to continue.

• **Vulgarities and character assassination are not permitted.** Try to establish ahead of time that mutual respect is expected. If the other person says something rude, you might firmly and cheerfully say, "Of course, from now on we are going to be on our best behavior and not resort to personal attacks." Insults and malicious remarks are off-limits.

• **Focus on the issue at hand.** Many people get sidetracked, sometimes accidentally, sometimes on purpose. Bring the conversation back on topic at your first opportunity. You might say, "In the interest of using our time together effectively, I'd like to return to the reason why we are here."

• **Negotiate in good faith.** There must be an implicit understanding that each person will explore several options as they communicate together.

• **If the discussion gets heated, say, "Stop!"** (See the discussion about this technique in step 6, Never Wave a Red Flag at a Raging Bully.)

In an ideal world, you and the person you are confronting will both agree to use the seven essential steps to managing conflict effectively from Chapter 6. A written agreement promising this would be invaluable.

If the other person is not capable of carrying on a respectful discussion, try the techniques from Chapter 10, "How to Handle Conflict Sabotage." If the other person insists on arguing, say, "Let's talk another time." Agree to reconnect again in a few hours or days or as soon as possible.

Get to the Point: The Three-Sentence Rule

Plan what you want to say to open the conversation. One to three short sentences will suffice. Consider writing down your sentences and memorizing them ahead of time.

For the rest of the conversation, be succinct. Whenever you speak, say something worthwhile. This not only keeps the dialogue moving but also helps ensure you won't say anything you'll regret later.

The One-Minute Rule

Although conventional wisdom has long held that women talk more than men, the latest research indicates that men and women use basically the same number of words in a day. When you factor in chatty women, quiet women, chatty men, and quiet men, it isn't too surprising that the war of words ends in a tie.

I think it would be more interesting to measure the number of words each sex uses on different topics. My clinical experience indicates that women use up more of their words talking about relationships. In the minds of many men, discussing feelings will never be Topic A. They save their words for more important things, like the game last night.

My client Grace said, "My husband confronted me recently because he hates long-winded conversations. When a conflicted issue is bothering me, I want to talk about it, but he complains bitterly that I ramble on and on. Sometimes Bob gets so antsy, he paces the floor. After that he yawns and acts like he's bored."

Grace continued, "Lee, you won't believe what he did! He pulled out his watch and said, 'I'm making a one-minute rule. You have exactly sixty seconds to tell me whatever is on your mind and that's all you get because I'm not listening to any more fluff.'"

I said, "Grace, how are you managing the one-minute rule?'

She said, "Honestly, I love it, although I don't find it that easy. Bob is a great guy; he's good to me and I respect him. It makes sense for me to use the one-minute rule, whether I like it or not. Sometimes this is tough for me to do. I have to condense what I'm going to say, and that means I must get to the nuts and bolts of the matter in a few short sentences. But it's working out fine for us!"

I am not recommending the one-minute rule for everyone. But five to ten minutes is probably as much as many men can tolerate.

Opening Statements to Use

Your initial comments are crucial, as they set the stage for how your negotiations will fare. This is when you think in terms of partnership, cooperation, and goodwill.

Acclaimed facilitator Dudley Weeks, Ph.D., author of *The Eight Essential Steps to Conflict Resolution*, points out, "Just as there is no magical time or place that can guarantee success in conflict resolution, there is no one perfect opening for every conflict."[2] Weeks suggests using the following statement to open your negotiations:

I get the feeling we've been trying to defeat each other when we've dealt with our conflicts. Maybe we've spent so much energy working *against* each other we haven't had any energy left for working *with* each other. We've both got a lot of *positive* power to use in dealing with this problem, so maybe we can use that power *together*.[3]

I suggest an opening statement spoken in an affirmative voice: "I believe this issue is negotiable." If you mention that you have some positive ideas to share, that sets an optimistic tone and should pique the interest of the other person.

Following are some benign statements that will enable you to get off to a good start. These statements are clear and straightforward, and they let others know how you feel and what you want. In this way, you validate another's self-worth, and they understand what you are trying to convey.

Opening Phrases to Use with a Loved One
"I love you very much."
"I care about you—you are important to me."
"I don't always have to agree with you to love you."
"I'm really scared you will reject me, but I must tell you that . . ."
"I get upset when you put me down, so please bear with me when I say . . ."
"You don't have to be perfect—just be yourself."
"It's not a matter of who is right or wrong. All I need to know is that you love me and like me, warts and all."

Opening Phrases to Use in a Professional Setting
"This is really hard for me to say, but I wanted you to know that . . ."
"I feel awkward mentioning this subject to you, but . . ."
"I would appreciate it if you would hear what I have to say. I'll make it brief . . ."
"I have two conflicts that need to be addressed, so please don't interrupt me."
"After I've had my say, I'll be glad to listen to what you have to say."

Other Phrases to Use

My physician, John Waeltz, M.D., and I were discussing the title of this book, and he said, "When my wife and I have a conflict, we have favorite ways to defuse our differences and then we settle down right away." Dr. Waeltz suggests using the noncommittal phrase

"You could be right," the reassuring "Your way might work out just fine," or the amenable, "I would rather be happy than right."

Following are some other magical words and phrases that will immediately neutralize your disputes with anyone in your life.

"You are right."
"Yes, I agree with you."
"Yes."
"Sure."
"That's OK with me."
"I see your point."
"You have a good idea."
"This is acceptable to me."

Simply saying, "Uh-huh," is recommended because it lets others know that you are listening. Often that's enough to satisfy your loved ones, friends, and coworkers.

In *Social Intelligence*, Daniel Goleman writes:

Of the many factors that are at play in altruism, a critical one seems to be simply taking the time to pay attention: our empathy is strongest to the degree we fully focus on someone and loop emotionally. People differ, of course, in their ability, willingness, and interest in paying attention—a sullen teen can tune out her mother's nagging, then a minute later have undivided concentration while on a phone call to her girlfriend. . . . Simply paying attention allows us to build an emotional connection.[4]

The Compassionate Response

My client Lucille had been dating Leonard for almost six months. Although she had a crush on him, she was exasperated because

each time she saw Leonard, he spent at least ten minutes rhapso-
dizing about his idyllic first wife. He would repeat similar stories
every time the couple was together. Lucille learned that Leonard's
wife had been seriously ill and had died eighteen months earlier.
Leonard described how they were soul mates, how they had been
married for twenty-three years, and how much he loved their four
children.

Lucille said, "I love Leonard, but I'm sick and tired of listening
to him repeating the same thing over and over again about his
deceased wife. I want to keep dating him, but I don't how to get
him off this conversation and on to talking about something else
without being unkind."

I said, "Lucille, just let him know you understand. You tell
Leonard you are sorry his wife died and that it has been so difficult
for him."

Three weeks later, I met with Lucille and she said, "I'm happy
to tell you that the strategy worked! I told Lenny, 'I'm so sorry you
have had to deal with the death of your beloved wife. I know it has
been so painful for you.' I couldn't believe it when Leonard said,
'It's all right, Lucille. She is in heaven and I couldn't wish her back
with all her suffering and prolonged illness.' After that, he said no
more about his wife and we had a nice evening. Since then we've
had four more dates and he hasn't mention his wife's name again,
not even once."

I said, "The compassionate response works miracles. We all
need to be more empathetic when others are grieving. Most people don't know what to say."

In truth, I learned the compassionate response from Mark.
Whenever I was down in the dumps, he would say, "I'm sorry you
feel so bad." I appreciated knowing that he really cared about me
and how I was feeling.

If your conversation is not going the way you expected and a
compromise does not seem to be forthcoming, I advise using the

compassionate response. This is usually a safe way to break down the emotional barriers between people. I've seen people do an about-face when they finally made a heartfelt connection.

Precision Communication

Constructive dialogue is necessary if your purpose is to settle your differences amicably. Most of us are so accustomed to communicating poorly that we have a long way to go when it comes to learning how to get our point across.

Back in the eighteenth century, English statesman Joseph Addison said:

> If the minds of men were laid open, we should see but little difference between them and that of the fool; there are infinite reveries and numberless extravagancies that pass through both.

Everyone has a brain full of bright ideas as well as silly notions. The wise man knows how to select certain ideas for conversation, while the fool will say whatever enters his head.

In order to have forthright conversations that are not contentious, you must be clear and concise and make it easy for others to understand you. Unfortunately, however, sometimes your intended message is not the message that is received.

Never Begin a Sentence with "You"

The minute we start pointing fingers—you did this, you did that—people start feeling defensive. And the minute people begin feeling defensive, constructive conversation quickly goes downhill.

Do not use accusations that begin with "you." For example:

"You were mean to me. You hurt my feelings, and you should
know better."
"You verbally attacked me, and I hate you for that."
"You are so pompous; you think you've got all the right answers."

Communication is direct and easy to understand when you use
"I" statements. Then you are taking responsibility for yourself by
expressing yourself in simple words. For example, you might say,
"I think . . . ," "I feel . . . ," "I'm afraid . . . ," "I'm upset . . . ,"
"I'm stressed out . . . ," "I'm really confused . . ." Then you
explain what you mean by giving a very brief example, such as:

"I'm sad that I'm not hearing any feedback about this idea."
"I would really appreciate a yes or no answer."
"I hear you better when you are not mumbling under your
breath."

Precision communication is easy because each sentence is short
and to the point. Then the receiver doesn't have to guess what you
mean. In this way, you converse and confront in a relatively pain-
less way. When you speak frankly, there is no mistaking that you
are in control of yourself. I advise that you take a "less is more"
stance and say what you must say in as few words as possible. Keep
your communication simple and easy to grasp. And if your Conflict Antagonist friend gets nasty, then remember when in doubt,
don't retaliate and you will have nothing to regret.

Use Caution When Saying "I Don't Know"

The phrase "I don't know" often puts us and others in an awkward
situation because it has so many interpretations. "I don't know"
can mean any of the following:

- "I honestly don't know, and that's all I can say right now."
- "I actually do know, but I'm not telling."
- "I'm confused, so don't ask me any questions."
- "I'm depressed, and I don't want to discuss this with you."
- "I don't have enough information, and I don't know where I'm going to get it."
- "I'm lying, but that's not for you to know."
- "I'm not skilled in forthright communication, so don't bother me."
- "I don't want to think about it; just let me figure it out on my own."
- "Stop being so nosy; it's none of your business."

Because "I don't know" has so many meanings, you must think as Conflict Innovators do and assume that "I don't know" is a vague message and nothing more.

When you say, "I don't know," what exactly do you mean? Be aware that in your own conversations you are creating a little cloud of obscurity when you use this expression. What are you hiding? Personally, I recommend that when you really don't know, counseling is the smartest way to process your thoughts and emotions. You will find out what you don't know, and it can be gratifying when this happens.

Avoid Saying, "Yes, But . . ."

A word of caution: anytime the phrase "Yes, but . . ." is used, you can anticipate that negotiations will collapse into bickering. You must decide if you are prepared to give an inch. You must settle down and consider what is in the best interests of "we" rather than thinking selfishly about "me."

"Yes, but . . ." takes the spotlight away from what you want to accomplish. Notice that when you say, "Yes, but . . . ," you change the subject, and then you are vulnerable to the other person's verbal attack.

For example, Donna said, "I hope we can go to a movie tonight."

There was a pause. Then Neil said, "Yes, but you always want to see movies that I don't like."

Donna said, "What's the matter with you? I see the movies you want to see."

Neil said, "You're in such a crabby mood, maybe we shouldn't go out tonight."

Notice this conversation started to go south with "Yes, but. . . ."

The phrase "Yes, but . . ." is contradictory. The "yes" signifies the speaker is in agreement. However, the "but" signifies there is disagreement, negating any consent that was originally implied. Often what finishes the sentence is a caustic remark.

When you discard "yes, but" and substitute "I agree with you" or "I don't agree with you," your conversations flow with ease because anyone can readily understand what you are saying.

Avoid Saying, "If Only . . ."

This is another phrase that takes you down a dead-end street. "If only" refers to wishful thinking that is tinged with sorrow and regret. It calls attention to long-ago golden opportunities that never materialized.

For example, Donna said, "We need to have a serious talk about how much we can afford for a down payment on that cute house."

Neil said, "If only you hadn't been so fussy, we could have had our dream house for less money."

Donna said, "If only you hadn't procrastinated, we could have bought the house across the street. It was so convenient and the price was right."

Notice how Donna and Neil are recycling old issues. "If only" means you are living in the past, referring to lost opportunities. The only time "if only" serves a valuable purpose is when you are sifting through your current conflicts, reflecting on your past mistakes, and hoping to make changes in the here and now.

If you hear the phrase "if only" come out of your mouth, that is a signal to you to switch into a positive mode instead of a negative one. It means you must put a stop to defensive behavior and start being more accommodating.

Ask Questions to Help Clarify the Issues

You act responsibly when you politely ask questions or point out when you don't understand what others have said. Why make a mistake when you can get more accurate information? For example:

> "I'm not sure I understand what you mean."
> "I thought you said you weren't available next week."
> "Could you please explain again exactly what you want me to do so I can complete this job on time?"
> "Would you please give me more information about that?"
> "I'm not sure I understand exactly what you want me to do."
> "I would appreciate it if you would show me how to do this."

Women ask questions because they want to be informed. They are curious, they need help, and they want to know what is happening day by day so they can make plans. Plus, they detest being kept in the dark. Men are less likely to ask for assistance or information. Apparently, it's a matter of saving face. They don't want to look foolish by revealing their ignorance, so they stay in the dark. They miss out on a lot that way.

My client Ginger said, "I love Samir, but he has an annoying habit of pretending to hear me when I know he wasn't really listening. I'll say, 'Did you hear me?' and he'll say, 'Yes.' Then the next day I have to repeat myself because he wasn't really listening."

I said, "This is what I recommend. After you say something important to Samir, ask him, 'What did I just say?' Politely ask him to repeat what you just said. If he was indeed listening, he will have the answer. I would not advise using this technique for every word you say, but if the issue is important, you need to verify if he really did hear you."

Conflict Innovators practice precision communication. You be the leader and be responsible for yourself, and others will heed your words when you are gentle with them and in control of yourself.

Use the Sandwich Strategy

I have used the sandwich strategy for more than forty years; it usually produces positive results. This is how it works.

1. First, you compliment the person you want to confront. Usually, words of heartfelt praise are appreciated. It is always possible to find something positive to say, even if it is only a compliment about something the person is wearing.
2. Second, you pleasantly deliver your confrontation zinger in one to three short sentences.
3. Third, you conclude by complimenting the other person again. This time say something appreciative about how he or she is handling your conversation.

The sandwich strategy puts others in a good mood by validating them. By saying nice things to the other person, you indicate that your dispute is not personal and that the two of you can have a friendly relationship.

Practice Intentional Listening

Precision communication is important in preventing misunderstandings. Also crucial is intentional listening, which includes:

- Listening to the content of what others have to say without judgment.
- Noticing the tone in which another person is speaking. Does he or she sound whiney, frustrated, hostile, sorrowful, even glad?
- Observing how their body language does or does not mirror what they are saying. Many nonverbal clues—such as the arch of an eyebrow, a toss of the head, or the position of the arms—speak louder than words.
- Monitoring your own tone of voice and what you are saying.

A major reason why relationships become conflicted is that people do not hear each other accurately. Intentional listening takes considerable concentration in order to catch every word and phrase and nuance. You may not interrupt, and you must stay alert. You also must refrain from blurting out any remarks without thinking, even retorts when the other person is rude or surly.

You use intentional listening because:

- You are curious and open-minded.
- You are being polite.
- You want to catch new information you may not have heard before.
- You are trying to understand, especially when the other person is confusing.
- You wish to be sensitive to another's point of view.
- You appreciate how unique and different people really are.

- You wish to catch the emotions the speaker reveals.
- You want to show that you care.
- You want to hear what you have heard before, but with a deeper awareness, sensitivity, and understanding.
- You wish to resolve your differences and achieve closure efficiently.

Remember not to personalize everything you hear. Whatever others say, the situation is not all your fault. By words and deeds, each person contributes to making our relationships joyful or miserable.

Take a Break

Sometimes it's best to walk away from the confrontation for a little while. You might take a five-minute break to restore your composure or a twenty-four-hour break to ruminate about how to reach an understanding.

My clients Becky and Connor never expected to disagree over vacation plans, but here they were, completely exasperated with each other about something that was supposed to be fun.

Connor was itching to go to Mexico for two weeks, but Becky had in mind a one-week cruise through Alaska. Connor felt cheated because he thought Becky was being unreasonable. Becky, on the other hand, felt misunderstood and ignored. Connor pleaded that he was exhausted and he needed to go where he could bask in the sun. Becky countered that she didn't have any more vacation time left for the year so this was her only chance to go on her dream cruise. The partners clashed, and neither would budge. She wanted it her way, and he wanted it his way.

Connor and Becky wisely thought it best to put this conflict aside for a few days. During that quiet interval, Becky insightfully thought of a simple solution. Enthusiastically, she approached Connor, saying, "I was so ticked off, and then all of a sudden it occurred to me that I could take a week off without pay! How about that? Now we can have two weeks in Mexico."

Connor replied, "Thank you, that's great. I'm glad you figured it out because I thought our vacation plans would never work out."

I said to the couple, "Sometimes it takes time to work things out."

The case of Connor and Becky was not resolved by compromise but by taking a time-out to deliberate and come up with a solution that wasn't available to either party at their initial discussion.

If you feel you need to call a time-out during your confrontation, here are some phrases to use:

- "I can't give you the information right now, but I'll let you know as soon as possible. How about we take this up again in forty-eight hours?"
- "I'm convinced that when we settle down, we will find out where we stand on this matter. Shall we meet again in one week?"
- "When I know exactly what you need, I'm sure we can work it out. Can you send me your specifications, and we'll meet next Tuesday?"
- "I'll have to think about this. May I get back to you tomorrow?"
- "I don't want to argue with you right now, so let's reconnect this weekend."
- "I need to give more thought to each of our disagreements. When can we meet again?"

The rewards of confronting with confidence are many. You feel happy because you addressed a problem that has been bothering you, and now it won't annoy you anymore. You feel relief because your well-rehearsed words enabled you to reach a respectful compromise. You feel proud because you expressed your grievances without alienating others. Now you can bask in feeling good about settling your misunderstandings in an amicable manner.

Questions for Reflection

- Do you sometimes feel like you have no guts because you are too timid to confront?
- Have you felt ashamed because you were too scared to confront and negotiate?
- Do you often feel inadequate because you don't know how to confront?
- Are you catering to loved ones but not getting your just due?
- Are you feeling guilty when you think about retaliating, so you don't confront?
- Do you insist on settling the score by battling it out and making matters worse?

Journaling

After you have answered the six questions for reflection, write about how you imagine a sensible discussion would be if you sat down face-to-face with a loved one or friend.

Once you are on a roll, write about the exciting ways you can stretch your brain with clever ideas that you have garnered from this important chapter. Then write about what you have learned from this book. Now imagine how it would be if you were optimistic about settling your disputes. As you start to think like a Conflict Innovator, your inspired thoughts point you in a direction that shows you how to amicably resolve your disagreements. Then write about the potential outcome of such a worthwhile effort. Be patient and stay the course, and you will have much less to regret by

10

How to Handle
Conflict Sabotage

L et's say you took everything in this book to heart: you memorized the seven essential steps to managing conflict constructively, you planned your confrontation carefully, and now you are in the middle of your discussion. Suddenly the other person sabotages all your efforts by ceasing to listen, starting to yell, becoming sarcastic, getting distracted, giving you the silent treatment, or refusing to negotiate. Following are some techniques to help you deal with Conflict Sabotage.

What Should I Do When the Other Person Won't Listen to Me?

I had a lesson in selective hearing the other day when I was trying to communicate with the supervisor of the fellow who had incorrectly installed a replacement part for my alarm system. I wanted the items fixed, but I was having trouble communicating with the supervisor as I tried to explain by telephone what needed to be done. He just did not seem to be hearing me.

The company was responsible for the mistake, so the supervisor was on the defensive. I told him in a calm voice that I was angry about the way this matter had been handled, and I didn't want to hear any more excuses or explanations. He defended himself with . . . more excuses and explanations! Finally, for the third time, I firmly told him that I didn't want to hear any more explanations; I just wanted the installation fixed. Then I said, "I am hanging up now!"

By that time, my body was trembling, my heart was racing, and I needed to settle down. About ten minutes later, the district manager unexpectedly phoned me to reassure me that a repairman was coming to fix the installation.

I spoke cordially with the district manager, Dave, and this is what I learned: the entire conversation with the supervisor had been recorded. Dave apologized, and I was relieved to be vindicated. I said, "Dave, there are a lot of people who do not listen. I was upset because the supervisor wasn't listening to me."

Dave said, "It's selective hearing. People hear what they want to hear. It happens all the time."

I thanked Dave for his perceptive insights and told him that I would put him in this book. And thanks to his help, the installation was promptly fixed.

Later in the day I told this story to a friend, and she said, "I bet the supervisor didn't like to be told by a woman that he was wrong!" By this time, I needed a laugh because earlier I had shed a few tears.

People do not all have the same level of concentration or hearing ability. It's possible that the people who tune you out:

- Can't understand your language
- Think you are nagging
- Find it is tedious to listen and are too immature to make themselves pay attention
- Don't care what you have to say

- Are preoccupied with their own thoughts
- Are in a hurry to do something else
- Assume what they have to contribute is more important than anything you have to say
- Are bored, so they change the subject
- Don't want to get involved in an argument
- Are not interested in the same old conversations
- Prefer to talk about themselves rather than hear what you have to say
- Don't want to give the appearance of agreeing with you or forgiving you

Sometimes selective listeners will fidget, yawn, or even have the audacity to fall asleep!

If there is a lot of background noise (for example, a television is on somewhere, construction is going on outside, or you are eating in a restaurant), the other person involved in your constructive confrontation may truly be having a hard time hearing you. Ideally, you have already made sure that you are using the correct language, and you are having your discussion in a room that is free of noise and distractions. Poor listening skills compound any conflict, but the tumult of busy lives is no justification for auditory shutdown. If you are in a quiet setting and the other person still is not listening to you, he or she is being rude.

My client Gwen had a terrible time getting her husband, Daniel, to listen to her. For a long time she took this personally, but she finally decided her husband was just self-absorbed most of the time. I asked Gwen how she made sure Daniel was listening, and she said, "First, I use his name several times to get his attention. He is usually in some kind of fog, but I have noticed that people respond to their own names."

"You are so right!" I agreed.

"If I'm telling him something important, I ask him if he's listening. Sometimes I ask him to repeat what I just told him. If I get the feeling he is just going through the motions of listening without really paying attention, I simply stop talking."

I couldn't help laughing. Silence is a very effective tool.

I must admit that when others are obnoxious and rude to me, I can't remember a word they said. I can only guess this is my way of protecting myself. So many women I know have memories like elephants, and they can repeat word for word what was said to them weeks and months later. I must confess that I've never mastered that skill. In fact, it is difficult for me to accurately remember conversations exactly as they are spoken.

I attribute my selective hearing to a traumatic time in my life when I was in my midteens. My mother was so unhappy that somehow she managed to put on her welcoming smile in public, but at home, she would rant and rave because she was so miserable. When she needed to vent, I was targeted to listen to her woes. Truthfully, my mother's rambling would often go on for an hour or more, and I wondered if she noticed that my eyes glazed over. I deliberately turned my thoughts elsewhere as I vaguely heard my mother complaining in the background. This experience is known as dissociation, meaning that your conscious mind is split: you hear, but you don't listen. This was how I protected myself from the full brunt of my mother's distress. Only in retrospect do I now recognize that sadly, I had very little empathy for my mother. No wonder I developed shallow relationships with my loved ones.

Years later, I discovered that I wasn't really listening to Mark, even when I was in the same room with him. I heard fragments of what he was telling me, but the full impact of our conversation was lost to me. I woke up and recognized that I had very poor listening skills. Eventually, I realized I was shortchanging others as well as myself when I didn't concentrate on hearing the spoken words. I know that when I tuned Mark out, I was being lazy and not doing him justice. Today, as a psychotherapist, I make a point of carefully, purposefully tuning in to every word anyone has to say. In fact, I make a concerted effort to listen intentionally, even to lip-read if need be.

If you are having an important conversation and you sense that you do not have the full attention of the other person, I recommend that you simply stop talking. Eventually, the other person will notice the silence. At that point, you might say, "I just wanted to wait until I had your full attention."

You might be tempted to just keep talking, because it is embarrassing to have to call attention to the other person's rudeness. If the other person is not giving you his or her full attention, save your breath. Remember that he or she is being disrespectful and doesn't know any better.

What Should I Do if the Other Person Starts to Yell?

If the person to whom you are speaking begins to act aggressively, that is your cue to stay absolutely in control of your own behavior. Do not take the bait and start yelling back!

I have found that it is possible to calm people down using just your voice. When the other person gets louder, you speak:

- In a low voice (lower than your normal speaking voice)
- Very clearly
- Very s-l-o-w-l-y

As you continue to speak, pace yourself. Your voice will take on a hypnotic quality that will calm the other person down. Say phrases like:

- "I know you are having a hard time. Would you like to tell me why?"
- "I can see you are upset. I am willing to listen, so tell me what is going on."
- "Are you willing to share your troubles with me?"

Of course, your body language needs to show that you are in control. Eventually, the other person will get tired of being the only big baby in the room. Most people are perfectly capable of controlling themselves, but they may choose otherwise. Often they behave in a hostile and unreasonable way in order to overpower others. If you are not intimidated, then their ruse did not work, and they will be obliged to give it up.

What Should I Do if the Other Person Starts to Cry?

Although there is such a thing as "crocodile tears" (fake crying), in my experience most tears are for real. For this reason, I do not put crying in the same category as throwing a temper tantrum.

Tears are a normal and necessary release of emotion no matter the circumstances, conflicted or not. When we weep, we cleanse our body of toxicity. It is interesting to note that the chemical makeup of our warm emotional tears is not the same as that of the tears that trickle down our face when we slice an onion.

Tears are often misunderstood because there are so many different kinds: heart-wrenching tears, worrisome tears, angry tears, fearful tears, tired tears, hungry tears, bittersweet tears, and tears of joy. Our tears reveal complex emotions: hurt, sorrow, grief, guilt, anger, fear, loneliness, remorse, and regret. I have even been literally bored to tears.

The more comfortable you are with your tears, the less stress you will have when your conversations focus on sad situations. And the more relaxed you are with your emotions, the more compassionate your conversations can be, and that encourages healing broken hearts.

We each have a personal responsibility to tend to our own tears. When our tears are freely released, there is no need to feel apologetic, but most women automatically apologize anyway because it is an ingrained habit.

Generally, women are eager to release their pent-up emotions when they are worried, hurt, disappointed, and emotionally distressed. They feel better when they discuss their troubles with trusted loved ones and friends. It is relatively easy for most women to express their grief, humiliation, guilt, sorrow, resentment, and regret. As a rule, women have the advantage of being more adept at verbalizing their wants and needs.

This isn't so easy for men to do. Men rarely feel comfortable enough to show their fragile side and stuff their emotions inside instead. I was surprised to learn that men feel worse after they speak of their weaknesses and vulnerabilities. Most men prefer to talk about finances, politics, cars, sports, fishing, hunting, camping, ski gear, and anything mechanical (trucks, computers, rebuilding the garage, and so on) because that's what interests them the most.

Men are reared to be strong protectors. Little boys grow up being told, "Boys don't cry—be a man." As this message becomes internalized, it explains why so many men—and some women—become stoic. I've noticed that the prohibition against men crying in public is gradually changing, but it's a slow process. How much better off the world would be if men would cry without embarrassment rather than smashing holes in walls and causing more trauma and distress.

At times you may understand your own tears. Other times you may not be sure why you are crying at all. I advise that you never attempt to interpret the meaning of others' tears. Let people interpret their own tears, or leave the job to a professional counselor.

Take note that when anyone cries for whatever reason, you should try not to say, "Don't cry!" This might be construed as insensitive. Another phrase that might be construed as hurtful and unsympathetic is, "You'll get over it." Even if you think the other person is crying in order to manipulate the situation, take the high road and avoid saying, "Quit crying, you faker!"

You are not obliged to fix the other person's tears. It is enough to be kindhearted and gracious and to show your caring concern. If another's tears are disrupting your discussion, suggest a five-minute break, and get him or her some water to drink.

What Should I Do if the Other Person Gets Sarcastic?

In an ideal world, everyone would play fair. People would follow the ground rules for constructive confrontation and would never lapse into cynical, demeaning, disapproving behavior.

If someone treats you in a bitter way during your confrontation, first humbly check your own behavior. Did you do anything to incite this attack? Is there anything you could have done to prevent it? Is there any chance your own tone was dismissive or snide? Remember to keep your voice low-pitched and conversational, with no hint of sarcasm or contempt.

In his book *Social Intelligence*, Daniel Goleman notes, "Of all the sorts of stress, the worst by far was when someone was the target of harsh criticism and was helpless to do anything about it."[1] Mean-spirited, know-it-all criticisms are distressing and difficult to manage.

By banishing blame and criticism, you are doing significant damage control. Following are some phrases you can use to discourage another's sarcasm. In the face of conflict, these statements are deliberate guiding lights.

- "Please let's agree to stop criticizing one another."
- "I'm not playing *gotcha* games because that's a dumb thing to do."
- "Blame and criticism are disrespectful and devalue our relationship."
- "Blame accomplishes nothing except to irritate me."

In the event you want to offer feedback to others, politely ask this question: "I have a critique to make. Would you like to hear it?" This gives the listener the option to say yes or no. By the way, this question usually piques the other person's curiosity. Remember: blame and criticism are off-limits except when a specific critique is requested.

Dealing with Interruptions and Distractions

Lily and her business partner, Sherry, were trying to decide if they could afford the cost of a new truck, but the conversation drifted, and next they were talking about the price of repairing the roof. Then they talked about the best way to revamp their conference room and what kind of furniture they needed. By that time they had lost track of their original conversation.

For many of us, it is difficult to conduct a discussion without getting sidetracked. During a constructive confrontation, there is a time for creative brainstorming, and that is when you are trying to come up with a mutually acceptable solution. The rest of the time, you need to stay focused so you don't waste time and run the risk of raising more questions than you can answer.

Some people have ADD (attention deficit disorder), which means they are highly distractible. People with ADD are keenly observant, and their brains are likely to go off on tangents when they notice something interesting. Having an argument with someone who has ADD can feel like herding cats. Other people deliberately use distractions and interruptions to sabotage a constructive discussion. Continuous interruptions, combined with two separate agendas regarding a highly conflicted topic, can create chaos.

Following are some polite phrases to use when the other person keeps changing the subject:

- "That is fascinating, but to return to the subject at hand . . ."
- "I would love to hear about that another time, but right now . . ."
- "I believe our starting point for this conversation was . . ."
- "Just to sum up where we are . . ."
- "I'm enjoying hearing about this, but the sooner we return to our agenda . . ."

What Should I Do When the Other Person Gives Me the Silent Treatment?

The silent treatment is akin to stonewalling and is deadly because it brings your constructive confrontation to a halt. People are prone to stonewall when they are fed up with being persecuted, hounded, mistreated, and discriminated against by others. Sometimes stonewalling leads to estrangement, which is overwhelmingly heartwrenching. Such an interminable breakdown in communication leads to a loss of contact for years on end. The incessant waiting tests the limits of our patience because there is no closure, making the ensuing grief extremely difficult to endure.

In his book *The Seven Principles for Making Marriage Work*, author John Gottman gives us a picture of stonewalling:

He tends to look away or down without uttering a sound. He sits like an impassive stone wall. The stonewaller acts as though he couldn't care less about what you're saying, if he even hears it.[2]

The person who stonewalls cuts off communication for a day, a week, or as long as a month for several reasons:

- He may be using silence as a way to punish you. In this case, it is manipulative, abusive behavior.
- She may be overcome with emotion and barely under control.
- She may think arguing is beneath her.
- He may be so distraught his rage is unrelenting.

Reaching out to someone who gives you the silent treatment is viable because he or she can still hear. If when you search your conscience, you discover that you have done something to provoke the silent treatment, then by all means apologize. However, I don't want to suggest that you deserve the stonewalling; this is not defensible conduct, and it is purposefully mean-spirited behavior. If you have followed the seven essential steps to managing conflict effectively, then you might want to approach the person who stonewalls—no apology required—and say:

- "I'm very unhappy that you have chosen not to speak to me. I have been trying in good faith to talk with you about this worrisome matter that is important to both of us. I appreciate your need for a 'time-out,' so let's take a break for a day or two."
- "I'm sorry if our conversation has caused you so much distress, and it is troubling that you stopped talking to me. It's

not possible to make progress on this issue when we are not communicating. Please understand that I'm still interested in working with you to reach a resolution so I'll call you tomorrow and hopefully, we can continue our conversation in a friendlier manner."

Inasmuch as the silent treatment is the antithesis of constructive communication, if the other person continues to refuse to speak to you, it's best to ride it out and seek professional help together, or the relationship may or may not be severed. What I have learned is that people are prone to change their mind when you give them enough time and space to rethink their hostile, contrary position.

What Should I Do if the Other Person Is a Control Freak and Won't Negotiate?

Control freaks insist on running the show. From the outset, their take-charge demeanor demands that you agree with them because they don't take no for an answer. In their self-absorbed way, they assume they are right and will go to their grave before they will admit their behavior is inappropriate. Control freaks believe they are right and you are stupid, and their polarized thinking makes it difficult to communicate with them.

It might come as a surprise, but in the real world, *you* most likely at times behave like a control freak. You might not know that others see you that way. Even the most mature among us will try to convince others, "I'm right and you're wrong, and nobody is going to tell me otherwise."

My client Fritz said, "I deal with so much incompetence at work that sometimes I have to take over to get the job done. The buck stops with me, so I don't feel I have any choice."

I've noticed many control freaks follow the rules they learned in childhood. Probably this makes them feel most secure. If their mother served dinner promptly at 6 P.M., then control freaks expect to do what their mother did. If their father compulsively made to-do lists, they grow up making to-do lists. If you don't follow the house rules, control freaks chide you for not doing things right. When they are irritable, their razor-sharp temper provokes many vicious arguments that deplete your energy.

Control freaks rarely, if ever, apologize for their mistakes, because their agenda is different from yours. Control freaks "sweat the small stuff," so when the least little thing goes wrong in their life, they view it as catastrophic. Control freaks have a superior attitude, but, paradoxically, this is because their egos are so deflated. Their need to assert control over everything and everyone is rooted in fear. Control freaks, more than anyone, realize how little control we really have in life. Their superior posture belies their deep-seated insecurities.

Control freaks grow up believing that they are entitled to have their expectations of perfection met by us, right now. There is no way you are going to be able to reverse a lifetime of this behavior. If you have the audacity to disagree with them, they stubbornly will not change their mind. You cannot sensibly argue with control freaks any more than you can rationally argue with a drunk.

Control freaks are interested in "me," not "we." They are self-centered because they are so rigid and scared, and communication focuses on their needs, not your needs. Much like obstinate little kids, control freaks don't want to do things your way. They are not interested in compromise. You do not negotiate disputes with control freaks, because you can't reason with them.

In his book *Make Peace with Anyone: Breakthrough Strategies to Quickly End Any Conflict, Feud, or Estrangement*, David J. Lieberman notes:

No strategy can be effective as long as the persons are not responding with reason. If someone is emotionally charged, particularly with anger, the normal rules go right out the window.[3]

Inevitably, we expect more from control freaks and they expect more from us. When there is no common ground and neither party is willing to budge, the standoff is painfully distressing because we want to shake them, but we know better than to do that.

- Conflict Avoiders exert control by refusing to address their disputes.
- Conflict Fixers exert their control by telling others how to live their life.
- Conflict Goof-Ups exert their control by making us feel sorry for them.
- Conflict Antagonists exert their control by blaming others.
- Conflict Innovators know that controlling individuals are doomed to fail because nothing can be as tightly controlled as they wish. Conflict Innovators understand that a relationship with control freaks can be meaningful when we patiently listen to them, compassionately show an interest in their concerns, encourage them when they are frustrated, and repeatedly shower them with kindness and caring concern. Conflict Innovators know that it makes good sense to keep any malicious thoughts to yourself because you aren't going to resolve your conflicts by alienating others.

Relating to control freaks requires dignity, patience, and mercy. Don't even think about disagreeing with them unless you want to see a temper tantrum or have the door shut in your face. Your best course of action is to follow the seven essential steps to managing conflict constructively. If you ignore any of these steps, you are apt to invite even more torment.

If you plan to preserve your relationship, do not ruffle the feathers of control freaks. You must be cautious and *never* personalize your grievances with any control freaks. You are wise to bite your tongue, nod your head up and down, and say, "Yes," "Sure," "OK," "Uh-huh," and "Of course," otherwise you end up arguing with them and further aggravating your conflicted situation. It is not wise to contradict control freaks out loud, although you mentally disagree with them. Be prepared to lower your expectations, because no hard bargaining will do. It is better to make some concessions rather than endure further aggravation. Think about accommodation, constructive cooperation, and reciprocal agreements because conflicted relationships do not have to be a contest of wills.

The "You're So Smart" Strategy

The happiest possible outcome is when you can indirectly lead a control freak to the conclusion you desired all along. The best way to do this is by using their self-interest as bait. Think of reasons why the outcome you desire would make the control freak look successful, brilliant, philanthropic, or whatever the desire of the day happens to be.

There is an entertaining scene in the movie *My Big Fat Greek Wedding* when the women of the family conspire to make the paterfamilias reach a foregone conclusion as if it were his very own original bright idea. He is, of course, unaware that the women are playing him, and they get what they wanted all along by letting him believe it was his solution. Everyone wins.

The "I Need Your Help!" Strategy

Another way to work with control freaks is to solicit their help outright. Instead of getting caught up in the monotonous blame-complain loop or even resorting to wearisome criticism, the "I

Need Your Help!" strategy is designed to encourage teamwork without nagging, pressure, coercion, intimidation, bullying, or force.

This one brief sentence—"I need your help!"—gives control freaks an unexpected chance to feel important and to work harmoniously as "we," not just "me." With support and encouragement, control freaks usually enjoy being asked to help with team projects. Say, "I need your help!" Then say no more and listen for the control freak's reply. If his or her response is surly or inappropriate, then simply repeat, "I need your help!" a second and a third time. Appealing to other people's honorable nature gives them an opportunity to be your friend or to be a hero/heroine. Do not be put off easily. In one sentence, make one specific request for help. Do not pull out a laundry list of complaints.

The following polite statements are examples:

- "I would appreciate it so much if you could be respectful of me, and I will do likewise."
- "I would be so grateful if you would clean the bathroom. I'll tackle the kitchen. That would be a great help."

You don't need to beg, plead, or describe your heart-wrenching problems. You are dignified. You do not roll your eyes. You are not sarcastic. You observe if the other party is willing to be a team player. If so, you have an opportunity to discover what it feels like to be important to each other. If not, then you know this person is not willing or able to be a supportive friend.

You do not have to understand control freaks to be forgiving of their quirks. Remember, there is nothing to be gained by getting them all riled up. We are pleasantly surprised when control freaks show their supportive side, and they do, because they like to be helpful. Then the door opens up for us to communicate with them with our dignity intact.

Questions for Reflection

- Do you frequently raise your voice and yell when you are frustrated with others?
- Are you comfortable crying privately with a friend?
- Do you feel guilty when you weep in public places?
- Do you apologize for your tears because you are ashamed to show your emotions?
- When you converse with others are you consciously aware when you are sarcastic?
- Are you prone to manipulate the conversation by interrupting the speaker?
- How do you handle another person's distractions?
- Have you ever been accused of being a control freak? If so, how did you respond to this assessment?

Journaling

After you have answered the eight questions for reflection, write about how you manage your tears in the presence of your parents, siblings, friends, and coworkers or anyone else. If you discriminate how you relate to others when you cry, then write about that. Also describe how you relate to your partner, family members, or other close associates when there is a lot of yelling going on. And if you are playing tit for tat, write about what another person's yelling and sarcasm does to your nervous system. Take time to describe how you feel when a person won't listen to you or gives you the silent treatment when you have a need to talk. Make note if you are prone to distancing yourself from close associates when you are conflicted and distressed and write about that. Mention in your journal your impressions of the "You're So Smart" and "I Need Your Help" strategies, describing in what circumstances these techniques would be useful to you.

11

Achieve Peace of Mind

When the Wilson family first came to see me, I could tell we had work to do. Roy (forty-two, a successful financial adviser) and Helen (thirty-nine, a fourth-grade teacher) had been married twenty-one years. Their daughter, Molly (nineteen, in college), was having boyfriend problems. Benjie (sixteen, a high school junior) didn't seem to care that his grades had slipped to C minuses. The family's relationships were in chaos. Communication between Roy and Helen had come to a standstill because Roy would speak harshly to Helen, and she would get scared and shut down. Molly was sassy and having a hard time growing up. Benjie was a rebellious, sensitive teenager who was trying to grow up fast. I first met with each one individually, so they could speak freely.

Roy was agitated as he spoke. "My life is a mess. I am trying to be the father I never had, and it's nearly killing me. I try to be superhusband, superdad, superboss, and supernice to my clients, but I sure don't get any thanks from Helen. I certainly can't count on her for support. And my kids are driving me crazy! There is always so much quibbling going on with Benjie, and I'm disgusted with Molly. She worked for me part-time, and I thought I could count on her when I really needed her help, but instead, she walked off the job in a huff and said she was never coming back. Then she had the gall to take off with her old boyfriend. Five weeks later, Molly's back, and she's got yet another lowlife boyfriend. I'm like a time bomb waiting to go off. My life is out of control, and I don't know how to deal with all this conflict."

Helen sobbed as she spoke. "Roy's in a bad mood all the time. We can't talk without irritating one another. In public, we look like the perfect family, so no one would ever guess the uproar in our home. I try to overlook it, but Roy has a fit when things don't go his way. So I keep secrets; he doesn't know half the stuff that goes wrong. I could never tell him about Molly's pregnancy scare; I felt so lonely dealing with it by myself. Roy is full of himself, and all he thinks about is what he needs. He yells a lot, and I yell, too. When I don't agree with him, he has a fit. I get so rattled that sometimes I give him the silent treatment, so things are quieter, but it doesn't solve anything. My family means everything to me, and all I want is for us to get along so I can have some peace and quiet. I really think Roy wants a wife who loves him unconditionally. It's like our marriage is all about him, and he's not thinking about me or what I want. I'm the only adult in the house because I pay the bills, do the parenting, and make the major home decisions. I need help, but I'm afraid to talk to Roy!"

Molly fidgeted and behaved as if she didn't want to be in my office. "My dad is constantly complaining that whatever I do is wrong, and I get so mad at him I just want to leave. He thinks he's the only one who is hurting. He acts like I should know what he wants all the time, and then he gets mad when I don't do the right thing. I'm tired of trying to second-guess him. Besides, he doesn't know everything. Two seconds after I came back home, he was yelling at me. I don't think Dad really cares about me."

Benjie hesitated momentarily. He was wearing black clothes and black nail polish and had a surly demeanor. He seemed to have picked up some of his father's know-it-all attitude. "You know my mom and dad don't get along. They say the stupidest things, like 'don't drink alcohol,' when I know they both drink. I've always tried to stay out of my parents' hair, especially when they argue.

But things are different now. Since I started high school, my parents have been down on me. They don't like my friends because they judge people by what they wear and what their hair looks like. How superficial is that? And what's the big deal if I smoke a cigarette or have a beer once in a while? Everybody does it. They expect me to be perfect, and I just want to have some fun. I don't think my parents are fair."

Neither Roy nor Helen was aware of how they subconsciously modeled their own parents' ways of dealing with discord. When I spoke to the couple about this, Roy indicated that he hated his father's aggressive behavior, but he hadn't realized how closely he mirrored his father's antagonistic ways of addressing conflict. Roy was a carbon copy of his dad—callous and bombastic—and he turned off the people he loved the most. He was taken aback when I suggested that he was acting a lot like his father. I recommended to Roy that he model his mother's more patient and deferential stance. I mentioned that he might take a course in anger management and learn to control his hot temper. Roy was iffy and said, "I'll sleep on it."

Helen's parents routinely hugged and kissed one another and were affectionate with Helen. She felt nourished and loved. When Helen married, she had expected this kind of affection from Roy. He had been reasonably loving when they were dating, and she thought after they got married and he was more comfortable he would become more affectionate. She was sadly disappointed that her husband was so brusque and unwelcoming. She said, "I never heard my parents quarrel. If they did, it must have been in the bedroom after we kids went to sleep." Helen had never learned to speak up or confront. Disheartened, she said, "I am such a coward! Why can't I stand up to Roy? Why do I let him walk all over me?" Her nerves were raw. She was aggravated and scared, and she berated herself. She worried that she had failed to strengthen her marriage and steer her family clear of so much conflict.

Roy felt guilty because he wanted to have a better relationship with Helen and his children, but instead he felt alienated and he pushed them away. Helen felt guilty because she knew she didn't have a clue how to handle her conflicts with Roy. Both felt guilty because their relationship had gone astray, and they were perturbed that they had neglected to enforce more appropriate discipline with both their children. Molly desperately wanted the unified support of both parents. That meant that somehow she and Roy would have to stop bickering. Benjie felt guilty because, at some level, he knew his parents should be firmer disciplinarians and he was getting away with bad behavior and bad grades.

I reminded both Roy and Helen that conflicted family and peer relationships are a universal challenge. I told them it was normal to have misunderstandings and they would learn sensible ways to listen, confront, negotiate, and show empathy when family members were at odds with one another.

I explained the five conflict styles to Roy, Helen, Molly, and Benjie, and they perked up when I asked them to identify any styles that seemed to fit.

Benjie had an impish glint in his eyes when said, "Well, I guess I'm a Conflict Goof-Up because I've got everybody mad at me."

Helen looked puzzled when she said, "I'm usually a Conflict Avoider, but when I yell at Roy, I guess you can say that Conflict Antagonist fits me. At work, I'm a Conflict Fixer because I take a lot of pride in being firm with my students. I don't put up with any nonsense. In some ways, I'm also a Conflict Innovator. I've designed some special projects for the elementary grades, and the teachers and students appreciate my creativity. But I'm sad that my communication with Roy is inadequate. With him, I'm mainly a Conflict Goof-Up, so I'm really all five styles."

Roy frowned when he said, "I know that sometimes I'm a Conflict Antagonist." Then he paused and relished saying, "Yeah, but the rest of the family are Conflict Antagonists, too." Roy added, "The truth is, I'm a Conflict Fixer with my clients because I spoon-feed them and give them a lot of good advice. My clients love me because I can be patient and help them a lot."

Molly had been sulking, and when I asked about her primary conflict style, she curtly replied, "I don't know!" I knew she could be charming with her friends, but her disposition changed radically when she related to her family members. Molly finally addressed her most pressing conflicted issues. "Look, I'm just trying to exist in this family. I don't hear anyone standing up for me. Even Mom is on my back these days."

It was obvious she was upset and distressed, as her personal agenda was more important to her than defining her conflict styles. After Molly had her say, I looked directly at each family member and said, "It's true, we all are Conflict Goof-Ups some of the time," and I didn't press the matter any further. Instead, I asked the family, "Has anything happened recently that you'd like to discuss?"

Molly jumped in. "*Twice* I tried to talk to my parents about the fights I'm having with my boyfriend, but Mom and Dad were distracted with something stupid. It's like the garbage bill is more important to them than I am."

Roy was preoccupied. "Just an hour ago I had to fire my assistant. She just never got it together. I was hoping I wouldn't have to do that, because it's a pain to train someone else."

Helen said, "I guess I'm just generally on overload . . . not feeling up to par. I think I'm having some health problems, so I made an appointment to see my doctor."

Benjie was on edge. "I wanted to go to the hockey game, but I'm grounded. I was hoping maybe my parents would be nice and let me go anyway."

With so many conflicted issues on the table, I wanted the family to settle down. I had a two-phase strategy that I thought would perk them up. I said, "First, I want each of you to share one or two enjoyable experiences from the past. We'll take turns focusing on one or two positive memories."

Roy said he liked traveling with Helen because she was adventurous. He said he had always liked taking Molly and Benjie to the playground when they were little because they always had a good time, and he doted on Molly.

Helen talked about the times when the family went camping and they all sang along. Helen said that her children were most important to her.

Molly thanked her father for teaching her how to ice-skate and for sharing this sport with her. She also said she had always looked forward to Saturday mornings at the library when she was a kid.

Benjie remembered when he was five and his parents had taken him to his first movie. He turned into a movie buff after that and had been one ever since. Benjie thanked his parents for helping him with his homework when he was younger, even when he didn't want to do it.

As the family reminisced about happier times, their gloomy mood gradually lifted, and I noticed they became more considerate of one another. And then it was time to get them involved in the second part of the strategy.

I said, "As a family, you are so conflicted you can't see the forest for the trees. Now this is what I want you to do: silently repeat the following sentence, and nod when you are finished—'I care about me; I care about you.'"

I waited a few seconds and they all nodded. Then I said, "Now I want you to face each other and repeat these words out loud—'I care about me; I care about you.'"

The kids were very guarded. They went through the motions of saying the words, but they were careful not to get involved in the message. However, Helen started to cry, and I could see that her tears affected the rest of the family.

I said, "I would like you to do that one more time. Please say, 'I care about me; I care about you.' Please look at each other as you say it."

The family repeated the words one more time. This time Roy reached for the box of tissues so he could wipe his eyes. Benjie sniffed and pretended he didn't feel sentimental.

Helen said, "Of course I care about you! You know how much I love you all."

Molly was the next to start crying. She sobbed, "I hope so, Mom. Sometimes it seems like you don't."

Roy said gruffly, "Come on, Molly. You're our only daughter. And Benjie, you're our only son. We just want you to be happy."

Benjie opened his mouth to make a sarcastic rejoinder, but it didn't come out. When the chips were down, he did not want to be the one to ruin the family unity they all needed so much.

My eyes watered. I was touched by the way each person reached out with warmth and affection.

I said, "When we started, there were several issues on the table. Molly has been fighting with her boyfriend, Roy had to fire his assistant, Helen made a doctor's appointment because she isn't feeling well, and Benjie was hoping to get to a hockey game. I think we should spend some time discussing and honoring these issues all together. What happens to one of you affects all of you. In my view, you need to learn how to behave like a caring family, not just four people who share the same last name."

Benjie, the opportunist, jumped in right away. "So can we discuss my hockey tickets first?"

I replied, "I am not going to make that decision. You are, as a family. For too long the four of you have been running on your separate agendas. It's time for you to start making family decisions. That means you reach a decision everyone supports or at least can live with."

I won't take you through the whole discussion about the hockey tickets, Molly's boyfriend, Roy's incompetent assistant, and Helen's appointment with the doctor, but I will share with you that as the family discussed these everyday issues, they began to appreciate that decisions made together were more likely to be equitable.

Also, because family decisions had the support of everyone, they were more likely to work.

The Wilson family had been sorely conflicted because each member had gone off in his or her own direction, thinking that they were all lone gunmen. In time they learned that making concessions for the benefit of the family meant a happier, more loving, and more secure home environment for everyone.

As I continued to work with the Wilsons, I shared with them my belief that caring relationships are built on the solid ground of the following:

- Abiding love—or, for people outside your closest circle, admiration
- Enduring respect
- Mutual trust
- Unfailing forgiveness
- Being frank and open and always expressing your truth
- Discussing major and minor decisions, so no one is caught off guard
- Talking about the best and the worst
- Allowing others to grow and not trying to control them
- Caring concern—being a help and consolation if there are setbacks
- Yielding without expecting to receive anything in return

Life Gifts

Inevitably, we are encumbered with contradictions: opposition and harmony, resistance and acceptance, struggle and surrender. Sometimes peace of mind seems to be more of a wish than a reality. In the following pages, I describe life gifts that will allow your relationship with others, as well as your relationship with yourself, to grow and flourish.

The Gift of Conflict

I know it is counterintuitive, but, as I hope you have learned, conflict is indeed a gift. Life is change, and conflict always changes the status quo.

In his book *Necessary Wisdom: Meeting the Challenge of a New Cultural Maturity*, author Charles Johnston presents an interesting perspective on what he calls living peace:

> Conflict and equanimity present the right and left hands of living peace. Peace without room for conflict offers not peace at all, but deadness, suffocation, and tyranny. The effective pursuit of peace in an integral sense requires that a person be not only tolerant of conflict, but understand its critical role in any creative process. If we reject our inner warrior, we will find ourselves facing its distorted image in our efforts at peace. In the name of peace, we will, in fact, wage righteous war.[1]

Johnston's words are especially important for parents. You already know from reading this book that conflict is an opportunity. If you insist on banishing conflict from your house, you are producing not peace but suffocation. When you allow your children to experience their own conflicts, they learn how to negotiate true peacefulness.

The Gift of Self-Sacrifice

Knowing that life isn't always fair, you would be wise to recognize and accept that circumstances will demand that you willingly make sacrifices for one another. These could be small and easily made concessions or enormous sacrifices of time and support. The abundant gifts of a strong supportive network of family and friends can help you through your difficult times. It is valuable to learn that sacrifice is not a selfless act if you take pleasure in doing something for those you cherish.

The Gift of Patience

In our hurry-up world, patience is often displaced with a pressing need for instant gratification. We don't want to wait, yet we must be patient because the laws of nature indicate that everything takes longer than you might have expected. I've noticed that Conflict Fixers in particular have a hurry-up mind-set. They make a lot of mistakes by thinking that their conflicted relationships can be resolved in short order.

It's true that we are always waiting for something: Easter, our birthday, high school graduation, finding the right mate, giving birth to a child, or winning the lottery. Whether you like it or not, you are obliged to wait because you don't know what will happen next. When you get impatient instead of taking life as it comes, then you are being unreasonable, because there is no specific deadline for when your differences will be resolved.

What should we do while we are waiting? The dual concepts of active waiting and passive waiting provide some simple answers. The following lists are adapted from my book *Should I Stay or Go?*[2]

Passive Waiting: "Poor Me." Passive waiting is a destructive process because people give no thought to the consequences of their conduct. The cost of passive waiting is tantamount to doing nothing but fretting in the face of unresolved conflict.

- Believe nothing in your life will change for the better.
- Remain negative; expect the worst.
- Be afraid of the pain of rejection.
- Lie to yourself—deny or minimize your traumas.
- Doubt yourself—say, "I don't know what I want."

- Blame yourself, others, or the fates for your conflicted predicament.
- Believe you are inadequate and helpless to help yourself.
- Get a multitude of opinions—stay confused.
- Do not trust your hunches; devalue your own judgment.
- See yourself and your life as not important.
- Be bitter, but don't ask for support or help.
- Remain "spiritually bankrupt."

Active Waiting: "My Time Will Come." Active waiting is a constructive, proactive process that helps you learn the high art of patience as you make a positive investment in your future. During this period you say, "I am resourceful. I am creative. I can persist. I can hang in there." When you diligently put active waiting into practice, you are on the path to gaining many new insights and making transformation a living reality.

- Admit that you are impatient
- Accept that your life is a work in progress.
- Look at waiting as a period of incubation.
- Understand that incubation is the void where something is percolating.
- Be aware that this void can last weeks, months, or even years.
- Recognize your frustration at being obliged to wait.
- Then immediately make a quick 180-degree shift and focus on a meaningful goal you would be proud to achieve.
- Feel your suffering when the going gets rough.
- Know that life's conflicted experiences are opportunities for new learning.
- Accept that no experience, good or bad, is ever wasted.
- Develop your spiritual faith.
- Patiently wait for the appropriate time and place to address your conflicted grievances in a loving, respectful manner.

The Gift of Acceptance

The gift of acceptance is tantamount to going the extra mile for others. Generosity of spirit begs you to be more tolerant because conflicted relationships are not particularly tidy. Allowances must be made for loved ones' idiosyncrasies, unconventional behavior, and special needs.

My client Becky said, "I had a low opinion of my mother because she was a falling-down drunk. Sometimes I drink too much, too, and I worry about becoming addicted. I admired my mom when I was a kid because she took my sister and me hiking in the woods, and now this is one of my favorite pastimes. It's hard not to be resentful, but I understand she had an addiction. I guess nobody's perfect—certainly not me."

Acceptance calls for flexibility and not trying to control another. Acceptance is incompatible with thoughts of revenge. You let your loved ones be right or wrong for them, while you are right or wrong for yourself.

Acceptance also extends to yourself. By accepting your own limitations, you have more compassion for other people. Think about how these qualities pave the way for you to accept those aspects of life that you cannot change. In truth, the more you accept that you are your own best friend, the more energy you have to focus on how you will address your immediate conflicted issues.

The Gift of Forgiveness

Why do so many people find it difficult to forgive an isolated error of judgment? Is there anyone who hasn't lost his or her temper, spoken too soon, or acted out of character once in a while?

True forgiveness is a gift that potentially strengthens the forgiver even more than it does the forgiven. Some of my clients tell me, "It is so freeing when I forgive the people who have hurt me." Forgiveness means that you let go of your mean-spirited emotions.

Forgiveness permits you to dispense with your fears and angers. Genuine forgiveness is a gift that strengthens your relationships. Forgiveness cannot be forced or hurried, but when you have the mercy and grace to forgive, then perhaps you might have a spiritual awakening. Rabbi Ronald M. Shapiro says, "Life hands us choices—will we forgive or avenge?" When you forgive, you are liberated and then peace of mind is possible.

Forgiving by rote is merely a sham. When you resort to shallow expressions of forgiveness, deep in your heart you know your message has a fake ring. There are times when you are so deeply wounded you might not want to forgive or when the harm done by another doesn't deserve forgiveness. But the risk of not forgiving might mean suffering sustained animosity, bitterness, and estrangement. When you are ready to forgive, then you let go of your resentment and bitterness.

Sometimes it is harder to forgive yourself than it is to forgive others. You might be down on yourself because you screwed up. You might set such high standards that you are burdened down with guilt when you don't meet them. Universally, it behooves you to be kinder to yourself and loosen your chains of guilt.

Facing life's conflicts with decorum is difficult when you have maligned others or when you have been maligned. True forgiveness enables you to negotiate fairly because you are liberated from the constant burden of guilt (if you cannot forgive yourself) or resentment (if you cannot forgive another).

Conventional wisdom says to forgive and forget, but you don't forget another's inexcusable behavior. The Dalai Lama has pointed out that if you forget, then you have no basis for forgiveness.

Rejuvenation and Prayer

Our lives are busier than ever. We go-go-go and don't take the time to smell the roses. My daughter, Laurel, said, "I've been living here sixteen years, and I don't know what my neighborhood looks like, so I'm taking walks and exploring where I live." We all need time to escape from our busyness. Our lives are often harried, and we need space in our day to meditate and restore our equilibrium so we can calmly address our conflicts in constructive ways. When you set aside your to-do lists and sing in a choir, act in a play, go for a walk, bake some bread, play a pickup game of ball, read, paint, or write, your life is enriched as you enjoy each day. Your rejuvenation time gives you an opportunity to recharge, refresh, and reflect. You find the energy to think creatively about your relationships and contemplate your conflicts.

There will be times when you are exhausted by your unresolved conflicts, and prayer can offer you solace and hope for new beginnings. However, when you have lost faith in humanity, then I suggest the "I don't know what to pray for" prayer. I know this sounds strange, but many of my clients have used it with remarkable success. They tell me it's better than feeling despondent and doing nothing about it. As one client said, "Well, at least I'm doing something to help me through my wretched turmoil."

The multiple benefits of the "I don't know what to pray for" prayer are time-tested, and the rewards can enrich your life. There are no set words for this prayer. At night before you go to sleep, address your higher power—whoever or whatever that means to you—and send your appeal out into the universe. When you are so tired and confused, and you don't even know what to pray for, ask to be given whatever would be best for you. When you pray for strength to persevere, you move from defeat and despair to hope and rejuvenation. Prayer is the balm that can make all the difference.

I also teach my clients an ancient Hindu mantra: "I am that I am." These words repeated several times are a powerful way to celebrate your personhood. In a firm voice, say, "I am that I am," three times a day for one week, and notice if you feel nourished with inner emotional strength. The more you reflect on these sacred words, the more you stay grounded. Personally, I feel a vital inner strength each time I say them.

My friend Reverend Dr. Linda Barkwill sent me an inspiring message from a Zen Buddhist text:

> The person who is a master in the art of living makes little distinction between their work and play, their labor and their leisure, their mind and their body, their education and their recreation, their love and their religion. They hardly know which is which. They simply pursue their vision of excellence and grace in whatever they do, leaving others to decide whether they are working or playing. To them, they are always doing both.

The Result: Sweeping Change or Baby Steps?

As you conclude your constructive confrontation, you do not need to pretend to be anyone other than your inexperienced, imprudent, and vulnerable self. It is not always easy to be certain you are saying or doing the right thing, but if your intentions are honorable and not malicious, your well-meaning attitude will prevail. Despite your imperfections and blunders, it is essential to love and respect yourself. You must make your own decisions, take responsibility for your own mistakes, and learn to trust your own judgment.

Note the following sentences and use them on a daily basis. Write these statements down and put them on the refrigerator door, in your wallet, or in some other handy place. Choose the sentences that are apt to improve your relationships and focus on them. Then say your favorite sentences out loud twice a day for three weeks and notice what happens:

- "I don't have to have all the answers right now."
- "I will change my ways of relating to my loved ones for the better."
- "I am doing the best I can right now."
- "I am willing to act with integrity and make one easy change at a time."
- "I am willing to stop arguing."
- "I am willing to do something different."
- "I will not despair if my adversaries are slow to change or don't change at all."
- "I will grow and energize my close relationships."

You might see small changes in your relationships but not take them seriously because you think they are a fluke. Think of each small change as a baby step. A baby sits before he crawls, then takes one or two steps and falls down, and one day walks across the room. You know that gradually, the child will walk, sprint, and run. Any change you make to improve yourself, your relationships, your family life, your workplace, and your community endeavors must be acknowledged. Your enthusiasm serves to stimulate and encourage you each step of the way, one step at a time. Then notice how much easier it is to resolve your differences. Be optimistic and encourage yourself each time you make a small change. It is fascinating to notice what happens next!

My former assistant, Elizabeth, had an arduous life story to tell:

My life was conflicted and unmanageable. I was married for twelve years and worked with my alcoholic husband, Artie, in his business. I was dissatisfied with who I had become—guarded, defensive, and fearing.

I've always believed in the power of prayer, but I wasn't aware that as I tried to take control of my life, I played both martyr and victim. Gradually, my health deteriorated, and intuitively I knew many of my conflicts were not addressed.

I felt miserable and hopeless, and it took major surgery to wake me up! I knew I had to take better care of myself. First, I read daily meditations. Second, I turned my life over to a Higher Power and practiced acceptance and gratitude. Third, I understood that my pain was a reaction to my past shallow life. I knew I had to make some radical changes and I did. I quit working with Artie. I stopped criticizing and nagging him because he smoked too much and got drunk too often. When I allowed Artie to live the way he wanted to live his life, I gave myself permission to do what I wanted to do, and that's when I went back to school and started a new career as a massage therapist. Eventually, Artie and I had an amicable divorce because I knew I had moved beyond reconciliation.

Mark and I were invited to Elizabeth and Tom's wedding. Sadly, two years later, Tom was diagnosed with a life-threatening cancer. Elizabeth was his ever-faithful, loving caregiver. Elizabeth said, "I stayed at peace with myself because I had been a hospice nurse for many years. And for so many years I studied and practiced so much self-care that I was able to stay serene during our awful ordeal. Every day I'm grateful for my life's journey and I'm grateful to the many loving family members and friends who supported us through Tom's final days."

I was often at the hospital to give Elizabeth and Tom my love and support. A few weeks after Tom's death, Elizabeth told me, "I have so many blessings. I am in good health, and I expect to keep on reinventing myself each and every day."

Elizabeth impressed me with her stamina, strength of character, courage, warmth, and loving care to all who have the honor to know her. She is an inspiration and a testament to the power of perseverance, patience, and a positive attitude.

I have developed the following credo to help all of us on our journey toward self-realization. Read or repeat this as often as you like, and it will settle into your unconscious mind, where it can begin to work its magic on your life.

I will take responsibility for my behavior.
I will demand less of my loved ones.
I will stop being defensive.
I will not permit my fear and anger to rule my life.
I will not hold grudges.
I don't need to have the last word.
I will not try to control others—otherwise, I do them a disservice.
I will listen to others with heartfelt compassion.
I will be forthright and tell others what I can and cannot do for them.
I will not always agree with everyone, but we can amicably agree to disagree.
I will argue no more because I want to enjoy my relationships.
I don't have to know everything to live a life of integrity.

The safest way to mend fences, if need be, is through counseling, patience, and letting time work on your behalf. Remember, by practicing the many strategies in this book, you put a stop to most of your conflicts before they have a chance to get started.

In closing, I hope you will be courageous and brave, make every day meaningful, keep the faith, and praise the powers that be that you are alive!

Epilogue

I have learned more about the complexity of conflicted relations by listening to my clients and paying attention to how I handle conflict. I hope you have learned and grown as you have studied the various ideas, concepts, strategies, guides, and rules that are intended to give you a better understanding of the many ways to address your disputes.

Now it's time to recall how you reacted when you first heard or saw the title of this book. I hope you have discovered much about yourself and how you and others address conflicts. Do you remember what you were thinking when you learned about the seven steps? Do you remember your first impression of the conflict styles? Now that you have completed this book, take a few minutes to reflect on any special understandings and insights that are important to you. Do you perceive conflict differently now?

Did you answer the questions for reflection and/or write in your journal? Was this easy or difficult to do? Do you know what issues you need to work on the most? Have you rehearsed and practiced any of the many strategies? If so, how have they worked out for you? If not, do you plan to use any of these skills when the time seems appropriate? Have you made any minor or major changes in your relationships or your life as a result of reading this book? Are you planning to reread this book for more information so that other insights and strategies sink in?

And are you aware of your own unfinished business? Be assured that change is in the offing for all of us one way or another. Personal growth is a challenge and well worth the effort. Did this book meet your expectations? Be it yes or no, I am interested in your stories and would be honored to hear from you. I can be reached at leeraffel.com.

Your interest in personal growth is commendable. I admire your courage and commitment to continue to do all you can to enhance your close relations. In closing, the best any of us can do is make every day meaningful and seek to achieve peace of mind.

Notes

Chapter 1

1. *Webster's New World College Dictionary, Fourth Edition* (Cleveland: Wiley Publishing, Inc., 2004).
2. Daniel Goleman, *Emotional Intelligence* (New York: Bantam Books, 1995), 130.
3. Coauthors with Julianne Holt-Lunstad on the study are Bert N. Uchino, Timothy W. Smith, Chrisana B. Cerny, and Jill B. Naeley-Moore, *American Psychological Association Journal*, Health Psychology.
4. Deepak Chopra, *The Deeper Wound* (New York: Harmony Books, 2001), 34.

Chapter 2

1. Douglas Stone, Bruce Patton, and Shelia Heen, *Difficult Conversations: How to Discuss What Matters Most* (New York: Viking Penguin, 1999), 59.
2. Marc Gopin, *Healing the Heart of Conflict* (New York: Holtzbrinck Publishers, 2004), 63.
3. Kerry Patterson, Joseph Grenny, Ron McMillan, and Al Switzler, *Crucial Conversations: Tools for Talking When Stakes Are High* (New York: McGraw-Hill, 2002), 37.
4. Definition of *criticism* from *Merriam-Webster's Collegiate Dictionary, Eleventh Edition* (Springfield, MA: Merriam-Webster, Inc., 2003).

5. Stephen R. Covey, *The 7 Habits of Highly Effective People* (New York: Simon and Schuster, 199), 34.
6. Definition of *projection* from *Merriam-Webster's Collegiate Dictionary, Eleventh Edition.*
7. Malcolm Gladwell, *Blink* (New York: Little Brown Publishing, 2005), 196.
8. Don Miguel Ruiz, *The Four Agreements* (San Rafael, CA: Amber-Allen Publishing, 1997), 57–59.

Chapter 3

1. Goleman, *Emotional Intelligence*, 4–5.
2. Barbara Kuczen, Ph.D., *Childhood Stress: How to Raise a Healthier, Happy Child* (New York: Dell Publishing Company, Inc., 1987), 309.
3. Erik H. Erikson, *Childhood and Society, Second Edition* (New York: W.W. Norton, 1963), 274.
4. Joyce L. Vedral, Ph.D., *My Teenager Is Driving Me Crazy* (Avon, ME: Adams Media Corporation, 2003), 59.
5. Lee Raffel, M.S.W., *Should I Stay or Go?* (Chicago: McGraw-Hill, 1999), 183.
6. Emily Brown, *Patterns of Infidelity and Their Treatment* (New York: Brunner/Mazel, 1989), 33.
7. Covey, *The 7 Habits of Highly Effective People*, 80.

Chapter 4

1. Patterson, et al., *Crucial Conversations*, 37.
2. Beverly Engel, *Honor Your Anger: How Transforming Your Anger Style Can Change Your Life* (Hoboken, NJ: John Wiley & Sons, Inc. 2004), 106–7.
3. Mark Sichel, CSW, *Healing from Family Rifts: Ten Steps to Finding Peace After Being Cut Off from a Family Member* (Chicago: McGraw-Hill, 2004), 69.

4. Lee Iacocca, *Where Have All the Leaders Gone?* (New York: Scribner, 2007), 5–10.
5. Marian Sandmaier, "The Road Less Traveled," *Psychotherapy Networker*, May/Jun 2006, 32.

Chapter 5

1. Roger Fisher, William Ury, and Bruce Patton, *Getting to Yes: Negotiating Agreement Without Giving In* (New York: Penguin Books, 1999).
2. Sichel, *Healing from Family Rifts*, 69.

Chapter 6

1. Patterson, et al., *Crucial Conversations*, 72.
2. Gopin, *Healing the Heart of Conflict*, 63.
3. Fisher, et al, *Getting to Yes*, 28–29.
4. Definition of *defensiveness* taken from *Webster's New World College Dictionary, Fourth Edition*.
5. Daniel Goleman, *Social Intelligence: The New Science of Human Relationships* (New York: Bantam Books, 2006), 215.
6. Gopin, *Healing the Heart of Conflict*, 286–87.
7. Sandra Blakeslee, "Cells That Read Minds," *New York Times*, 1/10/2006.
8. Goleman, *Social Intelligence*, 44–45.
9. Goleman, *Social Intelligence*, 215.
10. Ken Keyes Jr., *The Power of Unconditional Love* (Coos Bay, OR: Love Line Books, 1990), 12.
11. John Amodeo, Ph.D., *Love and Betrayal* (New York: Ballantine Books, 1994), 24.
12. Frank Pittman, *Grow Up! How Taking Responsibility Can Make You a Happy Adult* (New York: St. Martin's Griffin, 1999), 148.

Chapter 7

1. Goleman, *Social Intelligence*, 207
2. R. C. Fraley and P. R. Shaver, "Adult Attachment and the Suppression of Unwanted Thoughts," *Journal of Personality and Social Psychology* 7 (1997): 1080–91.
3. Amodeo, *Love and Betrayal*, 123.
4. Amy Sprague Champeau, *Amy's Well-Being Newsletter*, vol 4 issue 3 spring/summer 2007.
5. James F. T. Bugental, *The Search for Existential Identity* (New York: Jossey-Bass, 1976), 286–87.
6. Goleman, *Social Intelligence*, 44–45.
7. Fisher, et al, *Getting to Yes*, 22.
8. Ruiz, *The Four Agreements*, 63–69.

Chapter 8

1. Goleman, *Social Intelligence*, 247–49.
2. Amodeo, *Love and Betrayal*, 27.
3. Paul Krugman, "The Mensch Gap," *New York Times*, 2/20/2006.
4. Abraham Joshua Heschel, *A Passion for Truth* (Woodstock, VT: Jewish Lights Publishing: 2004), 19.
5. Heschel, *A Passion for Truth*, 104.
6. Suzette Haden Elgin, *The Gentle Art of Verbal Self-Defense* (New York: Prentice-Hall, 1980), 194–95.
7. Shakti Gawain, *Creative Visualization* (Mill Valley, CA: Bantam Books, 1982), 66–67.

Chapter 9

1. Fisher and Ury, *Getting to Yes*, 166.
2. Dudley Weeks, Ph.D., *The Eight Essential Steps to Conflict Resolution* (New York: Jeremy P. Tarcher/Putnam, 1992), 80.

3. Weeks, *The Eight Essential Steps to Conflict Resolution*, 80, 84.

4. Goleman, *Social Intelligence*, 50–51.

Chapter 10

1. Goleman, *Social Intelligence*, 230.

2. John M. Gottman, Ph.D., and Nan Silver, *The Seven Principles for Making Marriage Work* (New York: Three Rivers Press, 1999), 33.

3. David J. Lieberman, Ph.D., *Make Peace with Anyone: Breakthrough Strategies to Quickly End Any Conflict, Feud, or Estrangement* (New York: St. Martin's Griffin, 2003), 137.

Chapter 11

1. Charles M. Johnston, M.D., *Necessary Wisdom: Meeting the Challenge of a New Cultural Maturity* (Seattle, WA: ICD Press, published in association with Celestial Arts, Berkeley, CA, 1991), 68.

2. Raffel, *Should I Stay or Go?* 234–36.

Index